3/18/16
Pastors + Leaders Hea

The Rhythm of Faith

Jeneen Kohler

The Rhythm of Faith

ISBN: 978-1-942508-14-4 (softcover print)
978-1-942508-13-7 (hardcover print)
978-1-942508-18-2 (e-Book)

Unless otherwise noted, Scripture quoted taken from the King James Version.

Published by Touch Publishing
P.O. Box 180303
Arlington, Texas 76096 U.S.A.
www.TouchPublishingServices.com

Author photos by Diana Raines Photography

Library of Congress Control Number: 2015944707

Order additional copies through your local book retailer, through online bookstores, or directly from the author through Crowned House, Inc. at www.CrownedHouse.com

I dedicate this book to my children, Alyse and Bryce.
I give you these lessons learned as part
of your spiritual inheritance. May your lives
be marked by extravagant faith always.
I love you.
Mom

Table of Contents

Preface	1
Introduction	3
Chapter 1: Defining Faith	7
Chapter 2: Faith Requires Humility	25
Chapter 3: Faith Is Developed through Intimacy	43
Chapter 4: Are You Out of Your Mind?	55
Chapter 5: Faith Speaks	75
Chapter 6: Overcoming the Orphan Mentality	91
Chapter 7: The Stumbling Blocks of Faith	109
Chapter 8: Dream!	135
Steps to Salvation	156
Acknowledgements	167
About the Author	169

Preface

Ironically, I am writing this book about FAITH and I am finding it necessary to engage my own faith in order to begin. I feel afraid. I feel unqualified. I feel like no one will really desire to read what I have to share. Then, I remind myself that faith has nothing to do with my feelings! It has everything to do with trusting God's direction, standing on His Word, and moving forward in obedience. I love how Sarah Young defines faith in *Jesus Calling: Devotional Journal* (Thomas Nelson, 2013):

"Faith is the confirmation of things we do not see and the conviction of their reality, perceiving as real fact what is not revealed to the senses."

This is a long-awaited dream of mine. I have known for years that I will write many books, but it is always much easier to dream about something than to actually place my fingers to the keys and do it.

Obeying my Father is the highest priority in my life and He has commissioned me to write NOW! I guess He knew I needed the command or else I would talk myself out of this. However, because He has said, "BEGIN," I will begin and trust that His purpose and dream shall be fulfilled through me.

I believe it is a powerful thing to feel unqualified because ultimately that places all my trust in Him to accomplish this assignment. I press in by faith and denounce every hindering reason why I should continue to procrastinate this project!

My prayer is that whether you embark on reading this book as an individual, alongside a trusted friend, with an accountability partner, or as part of a small group study, you will take your time to allow Holy Spirit to speak to you. It is my experience that when God is teaching a new lesson or truth from His Word, He will support it in a variety of ways. That is my desire for you.

At the end of each chapter, I have crafted several study questions designed to enhance your learning. These are intended to:

- Guide you to deeper reflection on the scriptures.
- Identify personal application of the content in the chapters.

If you engage in this study as part of a group, I encourage the group leader to select from these questions to facilitate group discussion. Use the Prayer at the end of each chapter as a starting point in your conversation with the Father and to record the things on your heart.

FATHER, I TRUST YOU! Your enabling grace makes this process even possible.

Introduction

It was an ordinary weekday. I was steadily busy with the routine of domestic chores when I received a call from a dear friend. Answering just like I had for the past ten years, I was expecting a rundown of her weekend, or the usual things friends discuss: children, marriage, desires, dreams, etc. We walked in close fellowship with one another, learned from each other's journeys, and enjoyed life through much laughter. I had no idea that today's discussion would be anything different. A few minutes into the conversation, she made this friendship-changing statement:

"Jeneen, I can no longer be your friend because every day, as I look at your life, it is like looking into a mirror that constantly reveals the many shortcomings and failures of my own life. God does everything you ask Him to do and He just doesn't work that way in my life. I have come to realize that you are a pawn in the hand of God and I am merely a piece on the chessboard."

Her unexpected words slammed me to the wall. I remember the pain I felt inside as we parted ways. That was nearly ten years ago. Our parting caused me to seek God for answers. As I reflected on my personal spiritual life, I began to ask God to show me *why* my faith successfully prevails when placed in action? Is faith a special gift bestowed upon me? Do I have what is spoken of in 1 Corinthians 12? Is that kind of faith chosen for a select few or can we all walk in a lifestyle of faith?

As God began to give me clarity, I realized that sometimes a person truly is born with great talent. Let me explain. Celine Dion is a wonderful singer. She has been given vocal talent that is extraordinary. Yet, no matter how hard I try, I will *never* be able to sing like her. Although, seemingly everywhere I go, I am stopped by someone telling me I look just like her. I don't see it, but there must be some resemblance of truth to it because it has been a constant in my life for years. However, my looks will never create the talent this woman has. I could practice, practice, practice and still will never sing with her same clarity and power. She is a showcase! She is one in a million.

So often in the family of God, we see people this same way. We notice other Christians who seem to handle the pressures of life like a sturdy oak tree, those who seem to find revelation from God's Word with ease, or others who walk with inspiring faith. We notice the ones who appear to have it all together and we begin to compare our lives against theirs. When we come up short, somehow we decide to place this person on a pedestal to be admired as a showcase; something unreachable, unattainable. But, God is no respecter of persons.

Although it is true that we are all given different gifts and talents at varying amounts, God longs for *all* of His children to walk in the fullness of faith. It is not simply for a select few. It is the very foundation of the believer's journey. Faith is a mindset and a lifestyle we must train ourselves to operate in. But, beware! When we have walked with the Lord year after year, heard all the sermons on faith, memorized all the special verses, purchased all the good books, and believed for good things, we lend a dull ear to fresh and new insight. However, we must ask ourselves:

Am I seeing results through my faith?

In Ephesians 1:15-23, the Apostle Paul had this to say to the Christians in Ephesus:

"Wherefore I also, after I heard of your faith in the Lord Jesus, and love unto all the saints, Cease not to give thanks for you, making mention of you in my prayers; That the God of our Lord Jesus Christ, the Father of glory, may give unto you the spirit of wisdom and revelation in the knowledge of him: The eyes of your understanding being enlightened; that ye may know what is the hope of his calling, and what the riches of the glory of his inheritance in the saints, And what is the exceeding greatness of his power to us-ward who believe, according to the working of his mighty power, Which he wrought in Christ, when he raised him from the dead, and

set him at his own right hand in the heavenly places, Far above all principality, and power, and might, and dominion, and every name that is named, not only in this world, but also in that which is to come: And hath put all things under his feet, and gave him to be the head over all things to the church, Which is his body, the fulness of him that filleth all in all."

Jesus is all-powerful and because we have believed in Him as the Son of God and accepted Him as our personal Lord and Savior, we have become a part of His all-sufficient and all-powerful body.

Why then do we struggle to walk in His power? Why do we compare our faith-journey to other Christians instead of comparing it to what the Word of God teaches about faith? I believe it is because the power at work within us is activated by our faith and we cannot activate what we do not understand.

Paul did not say: I pray that "God" will become more powerful in your life. God is omnipotent. He is already all-powerful.

Paul did not say: I pray that "you" will have more power. It isn't more power that we need. As believers, we are already filled with all power.

Paul said: I pray that you would know (comprehend) and understand the power that is *already available* to you through Jesus Christ.

Potential

At the point of salvation, when the Holy Spirit comes to dwell on the inside of us, we are filled with all potential power to become. Seeds of potential ability, potential character, potential giftings, and potential faith are deposited within our spirits. We are filled with the potential power of God.

Notice the key word here is *potential.* It means, "The nature to become." Has anyone ever said to you, "Ma'am or Sir, I see a lot of potential in you?" What they are saying is simply this: the traits "to become" something great are visible on the inside of you, but you are going to need to first comprehend your potential and secondly, learn to work it, stir it up, and practice it.

Take the athlete, for example. Both of our children played several sports throughout their years of elementary and high school. Visible traits of the potential to become accomplished athletes were seen in both of them at a young age. Did those traits develop themselves? No! Alyse and Bryce spent countless hours practicing, sitting under the leadership of knowledgeable coaches, strengthening and conditioning their bodies, and building upon fundamental after fundamental until their potential became a visible fact.

Walking in the potential power that each believer possesses works in much the same way. That is exactly why Paul addressed the Ephesians using words such as knowledge, revelation, understanding, and enlightened. I believe a large majority of the Body of Christ is unacquainted with their potential in Christ. They are unlearned and living with untapped power.

This is why I am writing this book. It is my desire that at the closing of these chapters, your eyes would be enlightened. I pray that your spirit would receive revelation and you will know how to successfully activate all the power locked on the inside of you through FAITH.

Chapter 1

"Now faith is the substance of things hoped for, the evidence of things not seen."

–Hebrews 11:1

I AM AMAZED at the number of Christians I encounter who profess to have little or no faith. Does that surprise you? It surprises me because faith is the key element of the Christian life. And yet, when a Christian steps out and believes for something, and that something doesn't happen in the desired time-frame, he or she mistakenly lets that misplaced expectation of timing erode the faith that was initially present. Faith is called into question.

Just because something does not happen in your time-frame, that does not mean you do not have faith. Romans 12:3 tells us that God has dealt to "every" man "the" measure of faith. But what is faith? The biblical definition of faith is found in Hebrews 11:1: *"Now, faith is the substance of things hoped for, the evidence of things not seen."*

The New International Version says it this way: *"Now faith is confidence in what we hope for and assurance about what we do not see."*

The greatest faith a person can display was exercised the day you accepted Jesus as your Lord and Savior. Here's how I know: Have you ever seen Jesus in the flesh? Were you present at His crucifixion and resurrection? No, you weren't. Neither was I. There simply is no tangible evidence to build our confession of Christ upon. We make our confession "by faith" through the Spirit. It is our faith that becomes our evidence and gives us confidence of the very thing that we cannot see.

Hebrews 11:6 teaches: *"Without faith, it is impossible to please God."* Why? Because *"He who comes to God must first believe that He is God and that He is a rewarder of those who diligently seek Him."* You see, faith is a prerequisite to approaching God. It takes great faith to even believe that He *is* God. It takes mighty faith to pray to someone whom you have never seen and it requires more faith to believe that He hears you and that He has given you eternal life based on that belief. Just think about it! You have entrusted your entire eternity to a God you've never seen; but by faith He is able to be fully known. Fully felt. And fully personal.

Why, then, do you think it is so difficult to continue to trust that same God by faith for all things, every day?

I think the reason we question our faith is because we have reduced faith to an earthly virtue. We wrongly believe that our own firm resolve and determination can produce spiritual results. We believe that we must get into the right spiritual zone, conjure up enough faith by an act of our own will, and then try, try, try to believe for the impossible. That doesn't work because faith cannot be manufactured. It is received through reading and hearing the Word of God.

Faith Is Fueled by Hope

In the biblical definition of faith (Hebrews 11:1), we are reminded that faith is the substance of things "hoped" for. Hope is the joyful expectation of good–the confident expectation of a positive outcome. The hope you sense deep down in your spirit is an essential element to your faith.

You had hope for a better life the day you surrendered to Christ. You had hope that He could give you a better life than you had experienced thus far. Your hope led you to a place of surrender in which you placed your faith solely in Him for that better life.

Hope is the promise of eternal life. Your hope causes you to believe that goodness and mercy shall follow you in all the days to come. You find hope in the Word of God. True hope is a virtue that abides within every believer. It acts as an anchor to hold you in constant position to remain focused and steadfast in your faith (see Hebrews 6:19).

The earthly definition of hope describes it as a feeling. We must understand that feelings can be unstable, changing, and shaken. We often treat HOPE and LUCK as two auras that surround a person by chance. I refuse to use the word "luck" in my vocabulary. I do not believe that by some strange and unknown phenomenon I "fall into" good will and favor. No good or bad thing that takes place in my life is the result of happenstance, good luck, or bad luck.

I believe our lives are calculated and intentional. Our lives are the direct result of our ability or inability to understand God's kingdom. Yes, it is true that it rains on the just and the unjust, but even in trial, our ability to understand kingdom truths will result in joyfully going through the trial and entering a place of victory on the other side. We don't possess good luck. As children of God, we possess faith, favor, dominion, power, ability, courage, strength, joy, peace, and so much more. Our success and ultimate fulfillment in life will correspond to our ability to understand and abide by kingdom principles.

What hopes do you have tucked away in your heart? Do not be afraid to write down exactly what you are hoping for. The hope you sense deep inside your heart is from Holy Spirit. God longs to resurrect your hope and steadfastly anchor your life in it. He has beautiful plans for your life. Allow your hopes to guide you into powerful faith.

"But I will hope continually, and will yet praise thee more and more" (Psalm 71:14).

If you ever lose hope, you will lose the battle of faith because your faith is fueled by your hope.

Hope is the anchor that holds you in position to remain steadfast in your faith.

TESTIMONY

Unfortunately, I was not raised in a Christian home. At seventeen years of age, I became pregnant by my boyfriend of three years. I remember being so afraid. I had big hopes for my future, and being pregnant at seventeen was not part of the plan. Both of us had plans to go to college. As a result of our decisions, we were now forced to make a new plan. We married. Steve chose to forego college, get a job, and become our provider. I was left to finish my entire senior year of high school pregnant and the object of scorn. Hope was distant.

One Saturday afternoon, as I sat on the floor of our basement apartment listening to an Amy Grant cassette, I met my God. I can still remember Him wrapping me in His love and saying, "It is going to be alright." Just as I was, in all of my sin and failure, I was invited to come and enter into a relationship with the God of all HOPE. Suddenly, our circumstances began to look different and I was given the assurance of a bright future.

That was 27 years ago! God has been faithful to us and His hope continuously fills our spirits.

Faith Is Now!

I know it seems to be a small and insignificant part of the verse, but notice the word NOW in our biblical definition of faith from Hebrews 11:1. It is situated in the verse with grand significance.

Emphasize with me those first three words: "NOW faith IS!" Every second that you live is now! Stop for a moment and just allow that to sink in. We must live in perpetual faith that is uninterrupted and continuing indefinitely. Many believers exercise their faith only in desperate situations; in circumstances where only a miracle will do or in situations that feel out of their own control. But Hebrews 10:38 tells those justified in Christ to "live" by faith. That means we are commanded to continue in faith fueled by hope every single day, hour by hour, minute by minute.

"For I am not ashamed of the gospel of Christ: for it is the power of God unto salvation to every one who believes; to the Jew first and also to the Greek. For therein the righteousness of God is revealed from faith to faith: as it is written, The Just Shall Live By Faith" (Romans 1:16-17).

Did you know it is through the exercising of our faith that we are able to witness God at work in our personal lives? It is also through the exercising of our faith that God is revealed to the world around us. The Christian who operates in perpetual faith is a powerful demonstration to the lost world of a God who is alive and well today. Words often fail, but a true demonstration of faith exemplified through your life is clearly seen by all in your sphere of influence. It will set you apart and mark you as a true disciple of our Lord Jesus Christ.

Another important element of "NOW" faith is obedience. Do you know that it matters greatly what you choose to do right *now*? Obedience to God requires swift action now. Delayed obedience is DISobedience.

We learn obedience by the things which we are commanded to do. In other words, without laws there would be no commission of sin because there would be no such laws to transgress. So laws, rules, and statutes are put in place. As we submit to these, we act in obedience towards them.

As believers, we must cultivate an attitude of obedience toward God. This may seem strange to you, but when I was just a new-born believer, God spoke to my heart one day and told me to stop wearing pants. I was twenty-one years old. I know what you are probably thinking! "Oh, Jeneen, you probably went to one of those Pentecostal churches that command all of their women to dress that way!"

My answer to that would be "No, I did not." As far as I am aware, there was not one other woman in our church who believed she had to wear dresses every day. I will never forget it though. As I sat on the pew of a church I was visiting one Wednesday night, I clearly heard the command of God for me personally. I left that night and never wore another pair of pants or shorts for seven straight years. It was then that God lifted this conviction from my life and revealed to me that He had required this seven year season to teach me obedience.

Remember, we learn obedience by the things which we are commanded to do. Yes, I had a choice. In fact, I was twenty-one and in the prime of my life. While all my other friends dressed in cute jeans, I was the laughingstock of many while wearing my dress. But, I didn't care. I didn't HAVE to obey. It was my pleasure to obey. I love my God so much, and I knew He would never require something from me that wasn't going to work together for my good.

A short time later, God commanded me to homeschool our children. Although I am a teacher by nature, this was a huge sacrifice. While my friends simply dropped their kids off at school and had the entire day to cook, clean, and run errands, I was at home educating my children.

Oh, I hope I do not sound bitter. I absolutely loved home-schooling our kids. Those were some of the best years of our lives, but that does not mean it wasn't a sacrifice. By the way, God also required me to do this for seven years.

Friends, there is a vast difference between Jesus being Savior and Jesus being Lord. We love to acknowledge Him as both our Lord and Savior, but we are often mistaken in our understanding of how this looks in our lives. When you accepted Jesus as your Savior, it cost you absolutely nothing. However, to surrender to Him as Lord will cost your life. As you walk in obedience, you take on the very nature of Christ. The Bible says that even Jesus Himself operated in ministry as His Father commanded Him to (see John 12:49). I am fortunate to have learned obedience through the things which the Lord has (and still) commands me to do. Obedience brings blessing and reward.

"If you are willing and obedient, you shall eat the fruit of the land" (Isaiah 1:19).

As parents, we are fathers or mothers to each child the Lord graciously gives us, but reward and blessing comes to the children who obey our commands. This does not render our parental love conditional, though, because our love for our children never changes.

God's love for His children never changes, either. You cannot buy His love, nor can you receive more of His love by doing good deeds of obedience. However His blessing and reward rests upon the obedient. God loves all of us exactly the same, but through obedience we position ourselves under God's hand of blessing and favor.

I love the story of Abraham and his son Isaac recorded in Genesis 22. This is an amazing account of faith, obedience, and blessing. In the opening of the chapter, we read that God tested Abraham's obedience by commanding Abraham to sacrifice his promised son, Isaac.

"And Abraham rose up early in the morning, and saddled his ass, and took two of his young men with him, and Isaac his son, and clave the wood for the burnt offering, and rose up, and went unto the place of which God had told him. Then on the third day Abraham lifted up his eyes, and saw the place afar off. And Abraham said unto his young men, Abide ye here with the ass; and I and the lad will go yonder and worship, and come again to you.

"And Abraham took the wood of the burnt offering, and laid it upon Isaac his son; and he took the fire in his hand, and a knife; and they went both of them together. And Isaac spake unto Abraham his father, and said, My father: and he said, Here am I, my son. And he said, Behold the fire and the wood: but where is the lamb for a burnt offering?

"And Abraham said, My son, God will provide himself a lamb for a burnt offering: so they went both of them together.

"And they came to the place which God had told him of; and Abraham built an altar there, and laid the wood in order, and bound Isaac his son, and laid him on the altar upon the wood. And Abraham stretched forth his hand, and took the knife to slay his son. And the angel of the Lord called unto him out of heaven, and said, Abraham, Abraham: and he said, Here am I.

"And he said, Lay not thine hand upon the lad, neither do thou any thing unto him: for now I know that thou fearest God, seeing thou hast not withheld thy son, thine only son from me.

"And Abraham lifted up his eyes, and looked, and behold behind him a ram caught in a thicket by his horns: and Abraham

went and took the ram, and offered him up for a burnt offering in the stead of his son. And Abraham called the name of that place Jehovahjireh: as it is said to this day, In the mount of the Lord it shall be seen.

"And the angel of the Lord called unto Abraham out of heaven the second time, And said, By myself have I sworn, saith the Lord, for because thou hast done this thing, and hast not withheld thy son, thine only son: That in blessing I will bless thee, and in multiplying I will multiply thy seed as the stars of the heaven, and as the sand which is upon the sea shore; and thy seed shall possess the gate of his enemies; And in thy seed shall all the nations of the earth be blessed; because thou hast obeyed my voice."

Don't miss this truth: Obedience brings blessing.

TESTIMONY

In May of 2013, my family and I stood at what I refer to as a "Red Sea" sort of crossroads. We were desperately in need of God's grace in order to prevail and see our daughter successfully walk on dry ground to the other side. Today we stand on the side of VICTORY! The cries of joy and the celebrations are over, but the lessons I learned and the gratitude I have for God's amazing grace continue.

Once I became aware that we were facing a desperate situation, I immediately went to God in prayer. I prayed for four days with no release. I heard no answers and felt no peace in my heart for this particular request. It was as if a ceiling held my prayers captive. It was not until I began to make the eleven hour drive home to our daughter in Tennessee that I received a word from the Lord ensuring me of a victorious outcome. He plainly spoke, "I delivered Alyse back there." I had no idea at the time exactly what "back there" meant, but I clung to the promise of victory God was showing me.

Within days, God began to reveal His omniscience regarding our situation. He said, "You see yourself at the

Believers must cultivate an attitude of obedience towards God.

edge of the Red Sea needing deliverance as my people the Israelites did, but what they never realized was that I delivered them back there in Egypt. The crossing of the Red Sea was merely another obstacle that stood before them, but MY deliverance had already been provided. It is the same with your daughter! I delivered her back there and what stands in her way HERE is only a hurdle that I will help her to cross."

He showed me the "back there" place where He had delivered our daughter. I wept.

What I began to see was that God had delivered Alyse out of a desperate situation before any of us ever knew there was a situation. She did not even know! THAT IS OMNISCIENCE! So often, God reveals a situation to us and we begin praying about it. Somehow, we believe that when WE begin to pray, it is God's wake-up call to begin moving in the situation, but what God showed me was that He had already delivered and taken care of our daughter before we ever knew there was a problem to pray about! Do you see the faith we can have in our God? When God called us to prayer, He was simply choosing to partner with us. God can do it all by Himself. He is perfectly able. However, He chooses to co-labor with us.

Four days after the revelation that Alyse was delivered "back there," God gave me a dream. When I awoke, He gave me the interpretation of my dream, complete with instructions for the part I was to play for the next six days. The instructions were simply this, "Consecrate this day unto Me and in six days I want you to SHOUT and I will cause Alyse to cross this hurdle in victory."

I was out of town, staying with my mom. Together, we consecrated that day to God in fasting and prayer. On the sixth day, at exactly the moment Alyse was to be tested, we shouted together and God gave our daughter the above and beyond victory! Was I afraid of looking stupid? Yes, but I shouted anyway.

I feel a sense of vulnerability in placing this information before all my readers, but someone needs to hear this message:

- God has your life under control and in the palm of His hand, even when you are unaware.
- We are not always aware of His delivering hand. Sometimes, it is disguised in the missed test due to sickness, missing the bus, being late to the meeting, or whatever missed timing we perceive.
- Do not follow the instructions for another's deliverance. Seek God for the instructions He has specific to your situation.
- Only do what God says to do. Often we stress ourselves out trying to fast for 40 days and quote scriptures for hours. If that is the instruction God gives to you, then by all means obey, but there is a place of rest in the Lord while you wait. If all He requires is a shout on a specific day, then shout, my friend! Do not respond as Naaman did at first when he believed dipping in the Jordan River seven times to cure his leprosy was absurd (see 2 Kings 5).
- 1 Samuel 15:22 tells us, "Obedience is better than sacrifice." Remember this when seeking God's way.

I want you to know that you were created for victory. We were made to be overcomers in all things. Do not allow your desperate situations to keep you in fear and doubt. God has already delivered you "back there." So rest! If you are one of those who have put your faith in Christ as Savior, yet wonder if you have faith, I want you to know that it is not "little faith" or a "lack of faith" that holds you back. As God's child, you possess huge faith! Perhaps it has just been left untapped due to a lack of revelation and understanding.

May your lifestyle be marked by extravagant faith! You are full of powerful faith!

1. According to Hebrews 11:1, what is the biblical definition of "faith"?

2. Can you think of a time when you believed strongly for something and it did not happen? How did you feel?

3. Do you compare your faith against the faith of other believers? In what circumstances?

4. Remember that while it can be profitable to learn from fellow believers, each of us is uniquely created and formed for different purposes. It is not healthy to compare ourselves to another brother or sister in Christ. Stop for a moment and ask Holy Spirit to reveal to you any unhealthy comparisons in your life.

5. In this chapter, I made the statement that the greatest example of faith was exercised through you the day you accepted Jesus Christ as your personal Savior. Does this realization encourage you as you consider your faith? If so, how?

6. According to Hebrews 11:6, what is prerequisite to approaching God?

7. Romans 10:17 tells us that: "Faith comes by hearing, and hearing by the Word of God." We have access to many sources nowadays to hear the Word of God. Circle the ways you currently seek to "hear" and that increase your faith as a result.

Bible reading or Bible study	Church services
Small group participation	Sunday School
Biblical teachings via podcast or internet	Conferences
Bible College / Seminary courses	Intercession / Prayer
Reading Christian books	

8. Hebrews 11:1 teaches that faith is the substance of things "hoped" for. Make a list of the hopes you hold in your heart at this time and make a list of the hopes that, for one reason or another, you let die. Pray and ask Holy Spirit to reveal if these hopes should be resurrected once more. List anything revealed to you below.

9. Many believers exercise their faith only in desperate situations or when circumstances seem beyond their control. According to Hebrews 10:38, how often should you engage your faith?

10. What does "Faith is NOW" mean to you?

11. Obedience to God requires swift action, NOW. Name a few personal ways God has required your obedience recently.

Delayed obedience is disobedience. If you have been disobedient to God, there is no need to beat yourself up about it. Repent, and ask Him to forgive you. Then, exhibit the courage to step out in full obedience to God, now. Remember, obedience positions you for blessing and favor.

12. 1 Samuel 15:32 declares, "Obedience is better than sacrifice." What does this scripture mean to you?

Prayer

Heavenly Father, I thank you that I am filled with potential for full and complete faith. I repent of any false beliefs that my faith was small. I now understand that I am responsible for both building and exercising my faith through hearing Your Word and responding to You in obedience. Open my eyes, Lord, to fresh revelation of Your Word and help me to understand the greatness of Your power that is at work within me. Give me boldness to trust You in every area of my life. In Jesus' name I pray. Amen.

Use the space below to write any specific prayer requests you have:

Chapter 2
Faith Requires Humility

"At the same time came the disciples unto Jesus, saying, Who is the greatest in the kingdom of heaven? And Jesus called a little child unto him, and set him in the midst of them, And said, Verily I say unto you, Except ye be converted, and become as little children, ye shall not enter into the kingdom of heaven. Whosoever therefore shall humble himself as this little child, the same is greatest in the kingdom of heaven."

–Matthew 18:1-4

A LIFE MARKED by humility is necessary for walking in relationship with Jesus Christ. No, I am not referring to any of the distorted and skewed definitions of humility you may have been taught through the years. Many Christians erroneously believe that in order to be truly humble, you must become poor, weak, and marked by feelings of inferiority. They think you cannot live in a nice house nor drive a nice car. Once, I was even challenged by another believer on the concept of saving money. She believed that having a savings account was displeasing to God–the account was equal to "hoarding" in her own limited understanding. Some have been falsely led to walk around shamefaced, perhaps even dressing a certain way or refusing to wear make-up or jewelry, in order to prove their humility. The devil is a liar!

1 Peter 2:9 (NIV) declares: *"But you are a chosen people, a royal priesthood, a holy nation, God's special possession, that you may*

declare the praises of him who called you out of darkness into his wonderful light."

Our Father is not *a* king. He is *the* King! That means you and I are royal sons and daughters. As children of the Most High God, our lives should be indicative of His royal position. Feelings of inferiority and worthlessness are not a part of God's DNA. The world is His footstool and He reigns in the full measure of love, power, and control. We have been given His full legal authority and mandate to exercise dominion throughout the whole earth. Therefore, we are equipped to operate from a place of divine strength–never weakness. We are the head and not the tail.

The fullness of the universe belongs to God and prosperity in every area is our grand inheritance. God's will is not for His children to live in poverty. When God called Abraham to follow Him in obedience, He gave Abraham a precious promise: "I will bless you and you shall *become a blessing*." I love what 2 Corinthians 9:8 (CEV) teaches us:

"God can bless you with everything you need, and you will always have more than enough to do all kinds of good things for others."

Abundance is God's perfect will. You and I are God's answer to this lost world. In Christ, we find the abundance and overflow needed to become a blessing to every need Holy Spirit brings across our path. I actually encourage you to establish a savings account. As God provides you with finances outside the realm of your own personal needs, place the money in this account and always be prepared to become "the blessing" to someone else as Holy Spirit provides you with opportunity.

When defining humility, the ideas in question are not power, wealth, or superiority, but rather the position of one's heart.

We have been taught to portray humility through outward appearances. However, true humility is more than what we do or wear. Humility is a positional mindset–one that places modest or low estimation on one's own significance and rank. The genuinely humble have a healthy understanding of honor. This involves the ability to submit to those who are above you in rank, position, and authority. This is precisely why Jesus Himself said, "Unless you be converted and humble yourself like a little child, you shall not enter the kingdom of heaven."

Little children do not try to be equals with their parents. Children recognize their rank and dependency on mother and father. They honorably and fully depend on them for love, affirmation, identity, daily food and shelter, protection, guidance, provision, correction, discipline, and knowledge.

We approach God, not as His equal, but as His sons and daughters. It is important to have a healthy understanding of our dependency on Him. He is Abba Father and He deserves our honor and humble affection. Just as it is with earthly children, it is our position as sons and daughters of the Most High God to fully depend on Him for love, affirmation, identity, food, shelter, protection, guidance, provision, correction, discipline, and knowledge. When your trust is placed in any other source to provide these keys needed for healthy living, you set yourself up for disappointment.

Pride will exalt itself and try to keep you from a rightful personal relationship with the Father, forfeiting the blessed life Jesus died to grant you. Pride will tell you that it is pure stupidity to place your dependency on God. Worldly wisdom encourages you to find your own way in life and to depend on no one. I recently had a conversation with a group of liberals who proclaimed that, "Anyone with half an education would never be so naïve as to trust in a historical, out of date book written more than 2,000 years ago, much less govern your whole life by it." I found solace in Psalm 1:1(a): *"Blessed is the man that walketh not in the counsel of the ungodly."*

In other words, blessed is the man or woman who does not live his/her life according to the counsel of the world. In order to truly walk and live by faith, we have to undo so much of what we have been taught by mere human understanding and worldly principle. True humility will shift our lives from *defiance against* God and His principles to *compliance with* God and His principles.

"Humility is the fear of the Lord; its wages are riches and honor and life" (Proverbs 22:4 NIV).

Servanthood

True humility will escort you into a lifestyle of servanthood.

Consider this passage from Matthew 20:20-28 (NIV):

"Then the mother of Zebedee's sons came to Jesus with her sons and, kneeling down, asked a favor of him. 'What is it you want?' he asked. She said, 'Grant that one of these two sons of mine may sit at your right and the other at your left in your kingdom.

"'You don't know what you are asking,' Jesus said to them. 'Can you drink the cup I am going to drink?'

"'We can,' they answered.

"Jesus said to them, 'You will indeed drink from my cup, but to sit at my right or left is not for me to grant. These places belong to those for whom they have been prepared by my Father.'

"When the ten heard about this, they were indignant with the two brothers. Jesus called them together and said, 'You know that the rulers of the Gentiles lord it over them, and their high officials exercise authority over them. Not so with you. Instead, whoever wants to become great among you must be your servant, and whoever wants to be first must be your slave–just as the Son of Man did not come to be served, but to serve, and to give his life as a ransom for many.'"

Jesus tells His disciples four words in this passage we would do well to remember: "Not so with you." The longer I walk with the Lord, the more I realize that kingdom principles work exactly opposite of earthly principles. Our world screams, "Me, me, me!" and, "Take, take, take!" but the kingdom of righteousness teaches us that if we long to be great in the eyes of God, then we must become a servant to all. Serving equals giving! Giving of one's self, time, gifts, talents, forgiveness, love, finances, smiles, right-of-way, and so much more. Being a servant does not indicate that you will not hold structured positions of authority over others, such as president, manager, pastor, etc. It means that when you are given the responsibility of these positions, rather than usurping control, you serve the people from a place of humility, attention, and care.

As I mature in my faith, I realize the beautiful power in the humble position of a kingdom-minded servant. No one in the kingdom of God is greater than another. When we grasp this concept, we will begin to honor and value every person in the Body of Christ and work together in unity toward a common cause. Then, the kingdom of God will advance!

1 Corinthians 12:12-26 as phrased in *The Message* gives us a visual example:

"You can easily enough see how this kind of thing works by looking no further than your own body. Your body has many parts–limbs, organs, cells–but no matter how many parts you can name, you're still one body. It's exactly the same with Christ. By means of his one Spirit, we all said good-bye to our partial and piecemeal lives. We each used to independently call our own shots, but then we entered into a large and integrated life in which he has the final say in everything. (This is what we proclaimed in word and action when we were baptized.) Each of us is now a part of his resurrection body, refreshed and sustained at one fountain–his Spirit–where we all come to drink. The old labels we once used to identify ourselves–labels like Jew or Greek, slave or free–are no longer useful. We need something larger, more comprehensive.

"I want you to think about how all this makes you more significant, not less. A body isn't just a single part blown up into something huge. It's all the different-but-similar parts arranged and functioning together. If Foot said, 'I'm not elegant like Hand, embellished with rings; I guess I don't belong to this body,' would that make it so? If Ear said, 'I'm not beautiful like Eye, limpid and expressive; I don't deserve a place on the head,' would you want to remove it from the body? If the body was all eye, how could it hear? If all ear, how could it smell? As it is, we see that God has carefully placed each part of the body right where he wanted it.

"But I also want you to think about how this keeps your significance from getting blown up into self-importance. For no matter how significant you are, it is only because of what you are a part of. An enormous eye or a gigantic hand wouldn't be a body, but a monster. What we have is one body with many parts, each its proper size and in its proper place. No part is important on its own. Can you imagine Eye telling Hand, 'Get lost; I don't need you'? Or,

You are only significant because of that which you are a part of—the Body of Christ.

Head telling Foot, 'You're fired; your job has been phased out'? As a matter of fact, in practice it works the other way–the 'lower' the part, the more basic, and therefore necessary. You can live without an eye, for instance, but not without a stomach. When it's a part of your own body you are concerned with, it makes no difference whether the part is visible or clothed, higher or lower. You give it dignity and honor just as it is, without comparisons. If anything, you have more concern for the lower parts than the higher. If you had to choose, wouldn't you prefer good digestion to full-bodied hair?

"The way God designed our bodies is a model for understanding our lives together as a church: every part dependent on every other part, the parts we mention and the parts we don't, the parts we see and the parts we don't. If one part hurts, every other part is involved in the hurt, and in the healing. If one part flourishes, every other part enters into the exuberance."

TESTIMONY

Serving comes naturally to me. God equipped me with a love for hospitality. I enjoy having company. Often, we have people streaming in for a month at a time. It brings me much joy to make each person feel special. Our second refrigerator is stocked with everyone's favorite drinks. Detailed grocery lists are compiled to ensure their favorite meals are served. All beds are stripped and sheets are clean and crisp for arrival. I love to buy fresh flowers from the market to arrange in one of my beautiful vases. Many prayers are prayed for a God-centered visit. It never fails that each person who enters our home makes some sort of declaration that they feel the presence of the Lord here. Some have expressed they even hear God more clearly when they visit our home. We have even had people walk in the front door and immediately start crying because they feel God's love so strongly. You see, when it comes to serving others, what matters more than the "act" is the "attitude" in which you do it. I have one of my favorite sayings hanging in the guest room:

"I've learned that people will forget what you said, people will forget what you did, but people will never forget how you made them feel." –Maya Angelou

A humble lifestyle is derived from a conscious understanding of our position in Christ. He is Lord and our authoritative headship. In Him, we have access to all power, but humble submission to Christ will always lead us into the position of servanthood. It is the true nature of Christ. Even though He was fully powerful, He humbled Himself to the position of a servant that God's will might be accomplished.

Humility and Faith

"OK," you may ask, "but how does humility pertain to my daily walk of faith? "

First of all, there is a need to recognize that you are not a one-man show anymore. Through salvation, you have entered into a covenant partnership with God. 1 Corinthians 6:19-20 (NIV) teaches: *"Do you not know that your bodies are temples of the Holy Spirit, who is in you, whom you have received from God? You are not your own; you were bought at a price. Therefore honor God with your bodies."*

Your daily walk of faith should always point you in the direction of the cross and back to the price Jesus paid through death and resurrection, bringing you once again into fellowship with your Maker, Almighty God. You have been created by God for a distinct purpose. Truly, you are no longer free to live and do as you please. Your position now is to daily search the heart of God and bring yourself into alignment with His purposes. While the freedom to make your own choices remains, as His follower, His will for your life should become your highest priority.

Secondly, we have a mandate to look to God for guidance and direction in all things. One of the first verses of scripture I ever committed to memory was Proverbs 3:5-6 (NIV): *"Trust in the Lord with all your heart, and lean not on your own understanding; in all your ways submit to him, and he will make your paths straight."*

Let's face it. As human beings, we can only see in part and know in part. Only God is omniscient. He is your all-knowing Father. Would it not be wise to consult His opinion regarding your life? Would it not be wise to seek His direction regarding your next step?

I am thankful that early in my relationship with Jesus He placed great emphasis on the importance of being in the will of God personally. A portion of scripture that grabbed my attention and caused me to allow God to shepherd my entire life is found in Psalm 139:13-17 (NIV): *"For you created my inmost being; you knit me together in my mother's womb. I praise you because I am fearfully and wonderfully made; your works are wonderful, I know that full well. My frame was not hidden from you when I was made in the secret place, when I was woven together in the depths of the earth. Your eyes saw my unformed body; all the days ordained for me were written in your book before one of them came to be. How precious to me are your thoughts, God! How vast is the sum of them!"*

I imagine the book sitting on God's shelf in heaven solely about the life of Jeneen Bullen Kohler. All of my days are recorded in it. It is my life's mission not to miss fulfilling a single day. Therefore, I place high priority on seeking God's direction and submitting to His plan and course of action for my life.

And guess what? He has faithfully guided me for 27 years. He has never led me astray. In fact, by His guidance, my family and I have navigated into territories we would have otherwise never ventured into. Because we dare to acknowledge Him in all of our ways, our lives are full of purpose and we are fulfilling His destiny for our lives. I cannot imagine my life without the guidance and direction of my heavenly Father. He is my Shepherd and indeed the lover of my soul.

As we partner with God to walk as His Light shines on our path, we have the great responsibility to relinquish control to Him. In our finite understanding, it is easy to determine how we think things should go. We size up all the earthly details and reason amongst ourselves that the situation will go this way or that way, placing limitations on God's plan. However, as we relinquish personal

True humility will shift your life from defiance against God and His principles to compliance with God and His principles.

control of the situation and invite God into our circumstance to have His way, we will be surprised with the outcome. True humility enables us to take our hands off a situation and allow God full control. This surrender signifies our deep trust in the Lord. When He witnesses our trust in Him, He is then free to move and act on our behalf.

I have a type-A personality and although I am a woman of big faith, I had to learn the hard way that my headstrong, take-control personality was never going to produce the results of faith I desired. I came to realize that either I could be in control or I could allow God to have control, but there could be no in between! I quickly learned that it was in my best interest to relinquish all control unto God, in whom there is no limitation of knowledge or power. When you or I decide to take control, we limit the end result to mere human ability, but when we submit our plans to God, we enable Him to place His "super" on our "natural," yielding SUPERNATURAL results which cannot be explained. When our self-made plans exclude humility unto God, we can experience failure, but when we are led by His direction and guidance, the appointed end is purposeful productivity–every time!

Let me ask you a question. Have you ever made a decision and it ended in failure? Do you feel like your life has been a series of one bad decision after another? Making bad decisions can prohibit you from walking in God's purpose year after year. Bad decisions are time wasters! How long have you been stuck where you are? My friend, relinquish control unto God and confess today that your control has not helped you, but rather it has hindered your progression of faith. Repent and ask God to take control. He is waiting to bless your life.

Now, do not misunderstand what I am saying here. God doesn't expect us to be His little robots. Even Proverbs 16:9 tells us, *"The mind of man plans his way, but the LORD directs his steps"* (NASB).

God certainly expects us to use our brains to make decisions and decide plans, but humility reminds us to place the plan before God in prayer and receive His green light before moving forward. By all means, put together a plan and then leave the carrying out of the plan to God. For example, I have desired to write a book for many years. Instead of simply sitting down one day and beginning to write outside of God's time-frame, I chose to surrender my desire to Him. In March of 2014, God spoke to my heart to begin writing. I obediently proceeded in April. Although I am doing my part, I am still humbly placing this project before God on a daily basis, asking Him to anoint my writing and to also bring the appropriate people needed to edit and publish this book. I have left all of these provisions to Him. You see, life truly is a partnership with God. We are not robots. We are children of God who recognize our position in rank. He is the Head! I am the daughter! And, I am blessed indeed by my heavenly daddy.

TESTIMONY

In April of 2014, I was given the invitation to minister in South Africa. It came from a dear mentor and friend of mine whom I highly respect. I have traveled to South Africa several times and have many dear friends there. These people are like second family to me. Surely God wanted me to walk through this open door? Feeling important, I jumped at the opportunity and immediately began making plans to travel in August.

I had no sooner accepted the invitation when I heard a still small voice within saying, "You didn't ask *ME* if I wanted you to go to South Africa." My heart sank!

In my own reasoning and desire, I wanted to go! I didn't want to hurt my friend who had graciously extended this invitation to me. I kept thinking of all the women I could refresh and impact. Everything seemed fine and profitable for the kingdom.

Humbly, I decided to make the invitation a matter of prayer. I presented my case for going to the Lord, giving Him every reason why I thought this was a good idea. He spoke very clearly to me: "Jeneen, you are welcome to travel to South Africa, but I will not be going with you."

Suddenly, I realized that I could spend thousands of

dollars and much time traveling, standing on stages, and trying to impact many people, but choosing this route meant that I would be riding solo, without the anointing and presence of God. Without Him there is no impact. Without Him, transformation is no longer possible. Without Him, I am only a shell.

I learned through listening to the heart of God that He had other plans for me right then. He commissioned me to focus on writing my first book. Yes, the one you are holding in your hands.

In our daily lives, we find ourselves busy, but what are we busy with? Are we busy with our own plans, agendas, and schedules or are we busy fulfilling God's plan for our lives? Is God with you or are you riding solo? You, too, have a book in heaven with your name on it. Have you recently opened it in the Spirit, that its pages may be revealed?

Seeking God's will requires us to separate the desires of man from the desires of the Spirit. Discernment is key. Every good idea is not always a God idea. It does not mean there is anything necessarily wrong with the idea. It may simply not be God's plan at the time.

Never underestimate the importance of humility. Without such, it will be impossible to operate in the fullness of faith and fulfill the will of God for your life because you will be determined to carry out your own course of action and willful, earthly desires.

1. According to Matthew 18:1-4, how do we become great in God's kingdom?

2. What false definitions of humility have you personally been acquainted with?

3. The devil does not want you to have a healthy personal identity because once you realize *who* you are, then you realize what you are capable of doing. 1 Peter 2:9 says that you are chosen, royalty, holy, and a child of God. What lies has your adversary spoken in your ears that are contrary to God's truth about you?

4. After reading this chapter, how would you define true humility?

5. Jesus Himself said, *"Verily I say unto you, Except ye be converted, and become as little children, ye shall not enter into the kingdom of heaven"* (Matthew 18:3). What is your personal understanding of this scripture?

6. In what areas of your life do you need to trust God like a little child?

7. Define *pride*.

8. In this chapter, I wrote that pride will exalt itself and try to keep you from a rightful personal relationship with the Father, forfeiting the blessed life Jesus died to grant you. Are there areas of your life in which you have been prideful before God? Pause and let Holy Spirit speak to you about them. Confess them to God now.

9. Read again 1 Corinthians 6:19-20 (found on page 32). What does it mean to you when the scripture says, "You are not your own"?

10. Through salvation, we have entered into a covenant partnership with God.
Define *covenant*:

Define *partnership*:

Do you feel as though you have been effectively partnering with God? If so, how? In what ways can you better partner with Him?

11. Think about Proverbs 3:5-6. Why is it important that we do not lean on our own understanding? Why is it important to acknowledge God in all decisions?

12. Make a list of a few people in our culture who would be called "great" and indicate why they are considered so.

13. Now, according to Matthew 20:20-28 (found on page 28), who does Jesus say is greatest in His eyes? ____________________

14. Serving = ______________

15. In what ways are you currently serving others?

16. In what areas do you desire to serve more fully? What are steps you can take in this area?

Sometimes, we can be guilty of esteeming certain parts of the Body of Christ as greater than others. Allow Holy Spirit to sow this truth in the deep soil of your heart today, once and for all: Every part of the body is necessary, purposeful, and must be functioning properly for the fulfillment of God's work in the earth. Do not compare your function in the body to anyone. Recognize the valuable part you have been created to play and then play it well and with joy.

Prayer

Heavenly Father, Your kingdom is like no other. It is uniquely set apart as a light that shines from a tall hill into the darkest places. Your kingdom can easily be recognized because it is clothed in love and humility. I confess any area of pride that has operated within my life, keeping me from the fullness of relationship and partnership with You. For God, You so loved the world that You GAVE! Flow through my life as I give unto others by serving. Teach me to value and honor each member of Your body. In Jesus' name I pray. Amen.

Use the space below to write any specific prayer requests you have:

Chapter 3

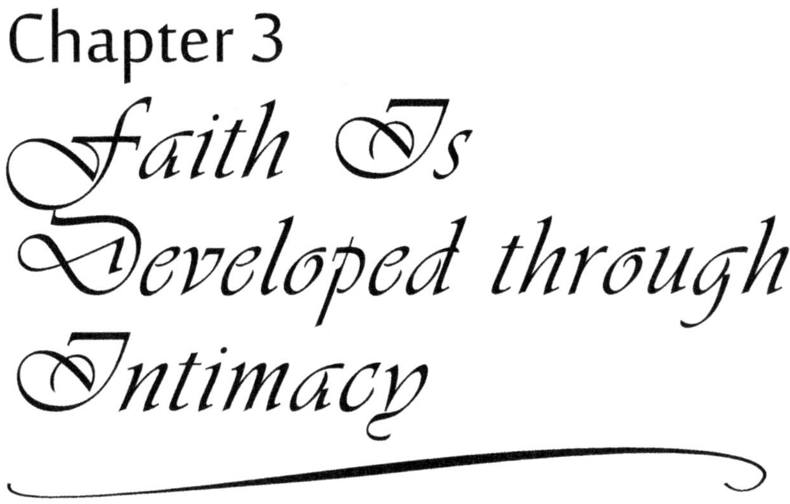

Faith Is Developed through Intimacy

"So then faith cometh by hearing, and hearing by the word of God."
–Romans 10:17

PEOPLE BELIEVE THAT you either possess big faith or you do not. Most do not recognize the fundamental truth that it is necessary to develop small faith into big faith. Everyone has been given the measure of faith–the seed of faith within–but it is your responsibility to grow your faith.

The Romans 10 verse above teaches that faith is developed by hearing the Word of God. Before we make any swift conclusions here, let us first determine what kind of "hearing" the Word of God is referring to. In order to fully comprehend, let us look at Matthew chapter 13.

"That same day Jesus went out of the house and sat by the lake. Such large crowds gathered around him that He got into a boat and sat in it, while all the people stood on the shore. Then, He told them many things in parables saying: 'A farmer went out to sow his seed. As he was scattering the seed, some fell along the path and the birds came and ate it up. Some fell on rocky places, where it did not have much soil. It sprang up quickly, because the soil was shallow. But

when the sun came up, the plants were scorched and they withered because they had no root. Other seed fell among thorns, which grew up and choked the plants. Still other seed fell on good soil, where it produced a crop-a hundred, sixty, or thirty times what was sown. He who has ears, let him hear'" (Matthew 13:1-9 NIV).

Are You Really Hearing?

First, this passage of scripture helps us understand that it is possible to hear the Word of God with our ears, but have no real comprehension of what we just heard. We also see that it is possible to hear and receive the Word of God with joy, but because spiritual immaturity, tribulations, and persecutions arise to work against the Word, we often get offended and neglect the truth we learned. Thirdly, we learn that one can receive the Word of God only to have it choked out by the cares of this world: lust of the eyes, the pride of life, and the chase for material possessions.

All three cases have one thing in common–the unwillingness of the hearer to intently "abide" in the Word. The type of hearing that is necessary to grow your faith is not only the kind of hearing you actively do with your ears, but also with your heart–in other words, your spirit.

James explained abiding in the Word this way:

"Do not merely listen to the Word, and so deceive yourself. Do what it says. Anyone who listens to the Word but does not do what it says is like a man who looks at himself in the mirror and, after looking at himself, goes away and immediately forgets what he looks like. But the man who looks intently into the perfect law [the Word of God] that gives freedom, and continues to do this, not forgetting what he has heard, but doing it–he will be blessed in what he does" (James 1:22-25 NIV).

Not everyone with ears is actually listening. Have you ever been talking to someone in conversation and they are looking right at you, but they are not fully hearing what you are saying? They only hear in part and, at times, they do not hear at all. I have actually engaged in conversation with people who are actively responding to the words I am speaking, but not actually hearing anything I say. After the conversation, they walk away, never remembering the words that were spoken. How can this occur?

There are several reasons why we can be in the presence of audible words and not really hear what is being said:

- We are disinterested
- We are preoccupied/distracted
- We are in opposition to what we hear

People truly hear when they value what is being spoken and are genuinely interested in it. If we are not truly interested in what is being talked about, there will be a disconnect between our hearing and our registering (receiving). Sometimes, we can really be interested, but our minds are focused on something else at the time. Perhaps we are distracted by some other event going on in our lives. Then, there are those times when we hear what is being spoken, but we don't like what is being said and we choose to dismiss the conversation.

It is necessary to train ourselves to intently focus upon and eagerly abide in the Word of God and not forget what we have heard through our spirits. Our faith contains the fuel needed to grow leaps and bounds when we eagerly and intently give full attention to the spoken Word of God. This type of attention and focus is referred to as intimacy.

Our faith grows and is made stronger through intimacy with God through His Word. Oh, I know what you are thinking! You thought intimacy was the act of sex between two individuals. In our culture, we hear of individuals having sex together and we refer to the act as "being intimate with one another." Contrary to popular belief, you cannot enter into intimacy through a one-night stand.

Intimacy is a product of quality time spent alone with another. Intimacy occurs when two people spend a lot of time together and become familiar with each other. As Christians, too often we want a quick relationship with God. We give Him little of our time and expect to receive all His benefits, but true intimacy is achieved through long association over a period of time. Spiritual intimacy is achieved as you become vulnerable and allow Jesus to speak into the deepest part of your life–your spirit.

Intimacy is a by-product of quality time spent together. Our faith grows when we become intimate with God through His Word and through prayer.

At the writing of this book, my husband Steve and I have been married twenty-seven years and we dated three and a half years before we married. Altogether, we have been in a relationship with one another for over thirty years. In thirty years, we have become quite familiar with each other.

I know Steve's character. I have learned what pleases him. What makes him happy. What he does not like. What he expects from me. I have learned I can believe what he tells me. In our thirty years together, he has proven to me that he is fully trustworthy. In all that I have gained through intimacy with Steve, it would be nearly impossible for anyone to come between how I feel about him and what I know to be true about him.

Like the intimacy produced over the years with my husband, I have learned the necessity of also being intimate with God. Years ago, the Holy Spirit granted me revelation of Matthew 11:28-29:

"Come unto me, all ye who labor and are heavy laden, and I will give you rest. Take My yoke upon you and learn of Me; for I am meek and lowly in heart and you will find rest for your souls."

Have you ever seen two oxen yoked together plowing a field? Consider the image below:

There is a purpose for the yoke that is wrapped around the neck of each ox. No two oxen have the same mind, will, or personality. If two oxen were placed side by side to plow a field, each would deliberately go his own way. The yoke ensures that the wills of these two completely individual animals be steadily focused on the same plan. Even if one desires to go his separate way, the yoke binds him to the task at hand–the straight forward plowing of the row. The yoked oxen work closely together and move in synchronicity to accomplish a common purpose.

"In the beginning was the Word, and the Word was with God, and the Word was God . . . The Word became flesh and made his dwelling among us. We have seen his glory, the glory of the one and only Son, who came from the Father, full of grace and truth" (John 1:1,14 NIV).

We know from these two verses in the book of John that Jesus is the Word of God. When Jesus compels us to come unto Him in Matthew 11:28-29 He is compelling us to come unto Him through His Word and learn from Him. He invites us to get to know Him, to understand His thoughts, and to learn how He works.

We have each been designed with unique personalities, desires, and wills. No doubt, we each have our own agenda and plan, but Jesus gives each of us a very special invitation to come and yoke ourselves to Him through His Word. He invites us to become co-laborers with Him in divine kingdom purpose. As we yoke ourselves to His Word, it acts as a bond that prevents us from pursuing our own agenda and instead coerces us to steadfastly remain focused on Christ's will and purpose.

As we commit to yoking our hearts and minds to His heart and mind found in the Word, we become Christ-minded. This yoking creates a close bond of intimacy that allows us to know Jesus personally. Knowing Him will cause us to trust Him and builds in us the inner desire to follow His plan for our lives. Allow God's Word to become your absolute authority. May it trump any situation, circumstance, or voice you come across.

TESTIMONY

Our son, Bryce, has desired to go and minister to the people of Sudan since he was 16 years old. Recently, at the age of 21, God opened the door for him to go to Kapoeta, Eastern Equatoria, South Sudan. In the months leading up to the invitation, I was privy to watch as Bryce sought the Lord about His timing for traveling to Sudan. I saw his tears and watched as he cried out to God for the Sudanese people.

So when God opened wide the door, I was not

surprised! I knew it could only be God to give Bryce such a desire to go and it could only be God to open the door at that exact time. Family members and friends panicked! Many voiced their opinions about the dangers of traveling to such a dangerous country as South Sudan. The internet was full of warnings, advising against travel to the country at that time. In fact, the American Embassy had been temorarily closed.

However, I was calm as a cucumber. How could a mother, the very one who birthed this child, be at peace with him going across the Atlantic Ocean to such a dangerous country?

GOD!

His plan had led Bryce to this fork in the road and He said, "GO." That was all I needed to hear. God's word trumps all fear and all worldly advice in my life.

By yoking to the Word of God daily, you begin to build an intimate relationship with Jesus. The more you get to know Him, the more you become like Him and begin to take on the very mind of Christ. This is important because in order to see results in your prayer life, you must pray for things in accordance with His will.

James 4:3 (NLT) teaches, *"And even when you ask, you don't get it because your motives are all wrong–you want only what will give you pleasure."*

Walking in partnership with Jesus is so much fun. I love how He actually places the desire to perform His will within our hearts. Recently, I have experienced a huge desire to move to Europe or at least spend quite a bit of time there. I am 44 years old and I can tell you that I've never desired to live in Europe. After I saw the movie *Letters to Juliet* I can testify that I desired to travel to Italy because the scenery in that movie was lovely, but just as quickly as the movie ended so did my desire. I guess most of us could say we wouldn't mind seeing the lovely Eiffel Tower, but to *move* to Europe? This desire is new to me!

I spoke to Steve about this crazy new desire I've had and, to my surprise, I discovered that he too was feeling pulled towards Europe. So, I began to ask God why we were feeling this way and He reminded me that in March of 2013 He had spoken directly to me, telling me that He was going to give me a victorious ministry in the nations of Europe. Friends, I had forgotten this. Do you see God at work here? He is filling my heart and the heart of my husband with the desire to spend time in Europe because this is His will for us. When you walk in intimacy with Jesus, God will begin to fill your heart with His special desires for your life. You will start to desire things you have never desired before.

In my younger days as a parent, I vowed that I would NEVER homeschool. Yes, well, you see what happens when you say "never." Truthfully though, in my own desire, I never wanted to homeschool. However, God gave me His desire of homeschooling our children because it was His perfect will.

Often, the reason we do not receive results to our prayers is that we have not yoked ourselves to the heart of God through intimacy. Therefore, our prayers are based on our own selfish desires and motives and God cannot fulfill that kind of prayer. He is not being mean. He is mercifully guiding your life and keeping you from the wrong path. If you feel as though your prayers rarely seem to get answered, check your intimacy level with Christ. Have you spent time getting to know His heart, what He likes, and what He desires for you? A conversation with someone involves a time to speak, but also requires a time to listen to what is being spoken back to you. As you train yourself to listen, you will begin to flow in a beautiful partnership with God that produces victorious results and joyful testimonies to your prayers. Trust me, the quality time you spend getting to know Him will be the most valuable investment of your entire life.

Rhythm Reflections

1. Have you ever known someone who you would consider to have BIG faith? What about them did you notice? How did their faith make you feel?

2. In what ways have you exercised BIG faith? What were the results?

3. It is Satan's job to discourage you. He uses discouragement to keep you from ever trying again. In what ways has he tried to stop you from operating in faith? Have you let him discourage you? How?

4. Satan knows that if you abide in an intimate relationship with Jesus, you will know the truth and be set free. That is why he tries so diligently to keep you busy. What areas in your schedule can be set aside in order to give quality time to developing intimacy with Jesus?

5. How do you feel when you are talking to someone and you discover they really aren't paying you much attention? The Bible contains the important words spoken straight from God. How do you think He feels when someone shows little interest in His words?

6. Before reading this chapter, would you have defined the word "intimacy" differently than you would now? In what ways?

7. Read again Matthew 11:28-29 (page 47). Reflect on what it means to you.

8. "The Word" is a living person. Who is it? ______________________

9. Do you see results from your prayer life? What can you attribute these results to?

10. Read James 4:3 again (page 49). Meditate on your prayer life. Can you say that you pray in accordance with God's desires or with your own selfish motives? Why is it important to recognize the difference?

11. What new desires is God filling your heart with?

Prayer

Precious Father, I thank You that Jesus Christ is the LIVING WORD and that He gives me a personal invitation every day to read the fullness of His heart and get to know Him in such an intimate way through the Bible. I ask You to forgive me for the times You have desired to speak to me, but I showed little to no interest. I want to know You in a very intimate way, Lord. I want to know You more than I know anyone else in my life. Help me develop a disciplined schedule that allows for time to converse with You every single day. I ask You to fill me with the desires of Your heart for my life. I desire to fulfill Your will. In Jesus' name I pray. Amen.

Use the space below to write any specific prayer requests you have:

Chapter 4

Are You Out of Your Mind?

"I beseech you therefore, brethren, by the mercies of God, that ye present your bodies a living sacrifice, holy, acceptable unto God, which is your reasonable service. And be not conformed to this world: but be ye transformed by the renewing of your mind, that ye may prove what is that good, and acceptable, and perfect, will of God."

–Romans 10:17

ARE YOU OUT of your mind? I am happy to report that I am out of my mind, indeed!

Walking by faith will always require you to be out of your mind. Allow me to explain. I have witnessed others attempt to walk by faith using their carnal minds. It doesn't work! Why? Because the fleshly, human mindset you were born with actively fights against faith.

Because we were born into sin, our minds start out in direct opposition to truth and the will of God. Romans 8:7 says, *"The carnal mind is enmity against God: for it is not subject to the law of God, neither indeed can be."* I guess you could say your mind has a mind of its own. Ha ha! Our sinful nature and mindset fight for control, lacking submission to God and His total authority.

Here is a newsflash for those of you who have been born of the Spirit: You no longer have to be controlled by your carnal mind! Unfortunately, many Christians still are because they do not understand the dire necessity for a RENEWED MIND.

I did not give my heart to Jesus until I was eighteen years old. So, as a child, my mind was ruled by fear. In fact, I slept in the bed with my brother until I was ten years old. Finally, at age eleven, my mother bargained with me that if I would sleep alone she would buy me a new bedroom set. I agreed and moved into my own room, but every night I was petrified. I would cover my entire head and body with blankets, leaving only a small hole exposed for my nose to protrude from and breathe. Do you remember the old, roll-down window shades? I had one of those on my bedroom window and I used stick pins to secure it to the window sill, ensuring that not one inch was left for anyone to peer through from the outside. Nightmares visited me with consistency.

It wasn't until I was in my twenties, married and living in Chicago, that I received victory over my fear! I will tell you how that happened later in this chapter.

Three Requirements for a Renewed Mind

Perhaps you do not struggle with a fear. Maybe it is insecurity that grips your heart; or condemnation, lust, envy, or doubt. It could be a multitude of things, but the cure-all is a renewed mind in Christ.

The Apostle Paul received great revelation from Holy Spirit about the need for a renewed mind among believers. In Romans 12:1-2, he addresses you and I and the Christians in Rome in this manner:

"Therefore, I urge you, brothers and sisters, in view of God's mercy, to offer your bodies as a living sacrifice, holy and pleasing to God–this is your true and proper worship. Do not conform to the pattern of this world, but be transformed by the renewing of your mind. Then you will be able to test and approve what God's will is–his good, pleasing and perfect will" (NIV).

1. Be a living sacrifice

The first thing I would like to note is the great apostle challenged us to be become as living sacrifices unto God. In other words, we must be alive and yet DEAD to our own fleshly desires, mindsets, and will. Now, I know what you are probably thinking.

Many people see our relationship with Jesus as one where WE have to personally give up everything in order to please Him. I have heard many people use this excuse as the main reason they do not want to live the life of a Christian. Religion has made our relationship with Christ a set of DOs and DON'Ts.

But, when you truly walk in an intimate relationship with Jesus, you soon understand that HE is your creator. He is the One who designed you and all of your intricate features. He knows what you like and what makes you tick. He created you for a specific purpose and He has plans to bless you and prosper you (see Jeremiah 29:11).

God is not out to steal everything that you love. Our Great God is a giver, not a taker! He desires for you to partner with His plan to bring you into wholeness and deepest fulfillment and joy. This is accomplished through surrender. It is what we call the Great Exchange. We offer to God our sins, our past failures, and mistakes and He offers to us forgiveness, grace, and mercy.

Shortly after committing my life to Jesus Christ, He lovingly asked me to give up watching my soap operas, R-rated movies, and listening to secular music. (He did not impress upon me to rid my life of these things because they were necessarily sinful, so do not allow my testimony to condemn you if you love your soap operas, R-rated movies, and secular music.) What God was doing in my life was graciously beckoning me to consecrate myself unto Him, separating myself in order to allow the necessary space for Him to speak! Ridding my life of the influences of secular music, R-rated movies, and soap operas afforded my mind a fresh beginning. It created room for Holy Spirit of truth to invade my space. Once again, we made an exchange. I exchanged these things that I enjoyed so much for a greater pleasure. . .TRUTH! This is a very important step in renewing the mind.

God is not saying "give up everything." Rather, He is asking you to yield all of your self-made plans, erroneous mindsets, fleshly desires, and habits unto Him and allow Him to sift through what is good for you and what is not. Once you really know Him, then you realize that this is not a punishment or a garnishment, but rather a huge benefit. He is merely asking you to surrender your entire being–spirit, soul, and body–and allow Him to reveal the BETTER way, the BETTER plan, the BETTER life that yields true happiness and joy.

Right now, perhaps you are saying, "But, I am *already* happy!"

Hear me on this: There is a huge difference between **happiness** and **joy**. Happiness is a human emotion that we experience when something in life greatly appeals to our senses. Happiness is circumstantial and conditional. For instance, I might be happy if I get a brand new beautiful car. However, that happiness can turn to sadness tomorrow if I wreck that brand new beautiful car. My happiness can turn to regret if I lose my job and can no longer afford the payments on that brand new beautiful car.

Joy can only come from the Lord. Joy is contained in your heart through truth and peace, and remains through any and all circumstances–with the new car or without it. Joy is not based on your circumstances.

Surrender your plans to God and you'll see that His long-term goal is to fill you with all joy, not with fleeting happiness.

2. Be transformed

Secondly, the Apostle Paul said, "Do not conform your life to this world, but rather *be transformed* by the renewing of your mind" (emphasis mine).

God desires to transform your thinking to line up with His. Years ago, Holy Spirit gave me this life-changing revelation. Man is comprised of three parts: **spirit**, **soul**, and **body**. You are a **spirit**, clothed in a **body**, and you have a **soul**.

Every human being is designed to worship his creator. Your spirit is the dwelling place of God within you. Until we surrender our lives to Christ, we are only partially living because without God, our spirit is hollow and void. When we accept the perfect sacrifice of God's Son and invite Christ into our hearts, Holy Spirit then abides within our spirit. We are not whole until we are filled with God's Spirit. When Holy Spirit resides inside of you, you are no longer your own (see 1 Corinthians 6:19).

Your **spirit** is a vital and necessary part of your existence. It is the only part of man that can commune with God. Now, I realize that when we worship or talk to God, we do this using our lips, or with a dance, or using another part of our physical self, but all true worship and communion with God flows from our spirit to His Spirit. That is why John 4:24 declares: *"God is a Spirit: and they that worship him must worship him in spirit and in truth."*

Spirit is the part of man that receives and comprehends revelation from God. 1 Corinthians 2:14-16 (NLT) provides us with this valuable information:

"But, people who aren't Christians cannot understand these truths from God's spirit. It all sounds foolish to them because only those who have the Spirit can understand what the Spirit means. We who have the Spirit understand these things, but others can't understand it at all. How could they? Who can know what the Lord is thinking? Who can give Him counsel? But, we can understand these things because we have the mind of Christ."

Your spirit is also the source of control for your soul and body.

The **soul** consists of your mind, your will, and your emotions. This includes:

- How you think
- What you desire
- How you feel

The **body** is the physical component of man. Though the spirit and soul of a man cannot be seen with the natural eye, the body of a man or woman is clearly seen. It is susceptible to the natures of the earth: physical harm, danger, sickness, and disease.

Because your spirit is the source of control for the soul and body, it makes perfect sense that the spirit should be the strongest member of your body. Without a healthy, strong spirit to rightfully control soul and body, we can sure get ourselves into a lot of trouble. If you struggle with unhealthy mindsets, bad attitudes, erroneous thoughts, and live on an emotional roller coaster, it is because you have allowed your soul to control your life instead of your spirit.

Have you wondered: "Why do I still have bad attitudes and

Transformation comes only through the renewing of your mind.

motives, struggle with addiction, and constantly live in a state of emotional instability? Doesn't 2 Corinthians 5:17 clearly state that once I have accepted Christ, I am supposed to be a brand new creature? Why then, am I still struggling with the same stuff I struggled with as a sinner? Am I not saved?"

Hear this: You DO love Jesus and you ARE a believer. You simply need a RENEWED MIND! Your new life will require you to "put off" some old things and "put on" new truths as you grow in the knowledge of the Lord.

Colossians 3:1-9 instructs us what we are to take off and put on. Highlight what you learn below:

"Since, then, you have been raised with Christ, set your hearts on things above, where Christ is, seated at the right hand of God. Set your minds on things above, not on earthly things. For you died, and your life is now hidden with Christ in God. When Christ, who is your life, appears, then you also will appear with him in glory. Put to death, therefore, whatever belongs to your earthly nature: sexual immorality, impurity, lust, evil desires and greed, which is idolatry. Because of these, the wrath of God is coming. You used to walk in these ways, in the life you once lived. But now you must also rid yourselves of all such things as these: anger, rage, malice, slander, and filthy language from your lips. Do not lie to each other, since you have ***taken off*** *your old self with its practices and have* ***put on*** *the new self, which is being renewed in knowledge in the image of its Creator"* (Colossians 3:1-9, emphasis mine).

How do we accomplish this "taking off" and this "putting on"? After I gave my heart and life to Christ, there was an immediate change of desires within my heart. As I grew by surrounding myself with other Christians and delving into the Word of God, my life took on a new appearance and new direction.

Still, in 2010, twenty-one years after my salvation experience, God spoke to my heart. He said, "The shaking has begun. IF you can walk with Me through this regeneration process, it will end in a place of power for you on the other side." The regeneration process He spoke of became a spiritual renovation in my life. God's desire was to take me to a new spiritual level, but in order to do so He needed to renovate my heart and mind. He began to tear down the man-made structures in my mindset and renovate my heart to love as He loves.

When Holy Spirit began to shine His light of truth in these areas of my life, I had to make a choice to *take off* or surrender these hidden places in my life to Jesus and *put on* the newfound truths.

This process lasted three years and required me to sit much of the time in isolation, away from everything I knew to be ministry. No one was calling on the phone requesting me to speak at their church functions or ladies retreats. After being VERY involved in the local church for twenty-one strong years, God brought me to a place where He would not allow me to step in to get involved or fill any needed positions within the church. He drew me all to Himself and renovated my life.

Take a refresher moment to allow God to speak to you on this matter. If there is anything you need to take off, take down, or take out of your life so God can put on the new self, ask Holy Spirit to reveal it to you. Go to a quiet place, take a walk, or just be still and listen for guidance.

I know now why He said to me, "*If* you can walk with me through this regenerating process. . ." The process isn't easy. Just as one renovates an old house by tearing down the old and replacing it with the new, God tore down a lot in my heart and mind. It was lonely, painful, and grueling. God desires to renovate all of His children. The question that remains is: Will you walk with Him through the regeneration process? One day recently, while reading the Word, I came upon this valuable passage of scripture from Matthew 19:28-30:

"And Jesus said unto them, Verily I say unto you, That ye which have followed me, in the regeneration when the Son of man shall sit in the throne of his glory, ye also shall sit upon twelve thrones, judging the twelve tribes of Israel. And every one that hath forsaken houses, or brethren, or sisters, or father, or mother, or wife, or children, or lands, for my name's sake, shall receive an hundredfold, and shall inherit everlasting life. But many that are first

shall be last; and the last shall be first."

One of the most powerful strategies I have found for "taking off" and "putting on" is found in 2 Corinthians 10:3-6 (NIV):

"For though we live in the world, we do not wage war as the world does. The weapons we fight with are not the weapons of the world. On the contrary, they (our weapons) have divine power to demolish strongholds. We demolish arguments and every pretension that sets itself up against the knowledge of God, and we take captive every thought to make it obedient to Christ. And we will be ready to punish every act of disobedience, once your obedience is complete."

As believers, we are responsible to fill our spirits with the knowledge and truths of God by reading His Word and developing an intimate relationship with Him. The more of Jesus we allow into our lives, the greater the transformation. This process is known as sanctification. Some say sanctification is a one-time, complete occurrence that happens at the time of salvation, but I find substantial evidence concluding that the process of sanctification evolves over a period of time for a believer. It is a calculated, intentional process that greatly involves YOU. You aren't just going to wake up one day and be a mature, whole, fulfilled believer.

"Beloved, I wish above all things that thou mayest prosper and be in good health, even as thy soul prospereth" (3 John 1:2). The health and welfare of our lives is found in the on-going prosperity and progression of our soul—our mind, will, and emotions. This is the key to true fulfillment and wholeness. This process of maturity takes place over periods of time, as we allow God to transform us into His image.

"Now the Lord is the Spirit, and where the Spirit of the Lord is, there is liberty. But we all, with unveiled face, beholding as in a mirror the glory of the Lord, are being transformed into the same image from glory to glory, just as from the Lord, the Spirit" (2 Corinthians 3:17-18 NIV).

I can say with complete honesty that I have been a believer for twenty-seven years now and day by day I am still being molded into the image of my Lord. The verse in John 30:30: *"He must increase in our lives and we must decrease,"* holds a valuable truth which allows my molding to continue.

When your carnal mind raises up arguments against the truth and wisdom that has been deposited in your spirit, it is your obligation and responsibility to bring those thoughts and arguments into captivity. In other words, lock them away in prison and resort to dwelling on the truth and wisdom you have hidden away in your spirit. The problem for many believers is that they have not taken the time to nourish their spirits. Therefore, when erroneous thoughts and arguments which are contrary to truth arise in their minds, there is nothing in their spirits to fight with. You will not be able to recognize the devil's deception until you fill your mind with truth. TRUTH alone will expose a lie!

Intimacy, time spent alone with God, is crucial to your everyday victory as a Christian and affords you strong faith to live by. Trying to live a victorious life void of intimacy with Christ and without a renewed mind is like trying to navigate across the country without a road map. God's Word is your road map for life. Everything you will ever need is found within its pages. It contains the directions to LIFE!

When we do not know what to do, we can ask God for wisdom. James 1:5 reads: *"If any of you lacks wisdom, you should ask God, who gives generously to all without finding fault, and it will be given to you."*

The spirit must be nourished by truth and wisdom. Wisdom is the supernatural ability to understand a situation from God's perspective, instead of processing it through earthly understanding. Wisdom is revealed through like-mindedness with God and deposited into our spirits.

Proverbs 3:13-18 shows us the real value of wisdom:

"Happy is the man that findeth wisdom, and the man that getteth understanding. For the merchandise of it is better than the merchandise of silver, and the gain thereof than fine gold. She is more precious than rubies: and all the things thou canst desire are not to be compared unto her. Length of days is in her right hand; and in her left hand riches and honour. Her ways are ways of pleasantness, and all her paths are peace. She is a tree of life to them

that lay hold upon her: and happy is every one that retaineth her."

In one of his famous sermons titled *The Fourfold Treasure*, Charles Spurgeon said, "Wisdom is, I suppose, the right use of knowledge. To know is not to be wise. Many men know a great deal, and are all the more fools for what they know. There is no fool so great a fool as a knowing fool. But to know how to use knowledge is to have wisdom."

The realization is this: One of the three parts of your life is going to be in control at all times. If your spirit is not the strongest part of your existence, then you will live according to the carnal beliefs of your mind or the fleshly desires of your body. There is simply no way around it. But, if you learn to live your life in the Spirit, God's Word declares that you will not fulfill or carry out the lusts and desires of the flesh (see Galatians 5:16).

The first ten years after I gave my heart and life to Christ, I was not aware of this principle. I suffered many attacks against my mind. I would often wake up to a dark cloud over me, whispering condemnation from daylight to dark.

"No one likes you."

"Look what you did yesterday."

"You messed up."

"You can't do anything right."

"You shouldn't have said that."

The condemnation, insecurity, and guilt remained until I began to fill my spirit with truth about myself from the Word of God. Remember, whatever you constantly feed will grow and whatever you starve will eventually die. I learned to feed my spirit and starve my soul and flesh of having power over me. In time, I became whole! I love what Hebrews 4:12 tells us:

"For the word of God is quick, powerful and sharper than any two-edged sword, piercing even to the dividing asunder of soul and spirit, and the joints and marrow, and is a discerner of the thoughts and intents of the heart."

When we read, study, and meditate on the Word of God, it acts as a two-edged sword that cuts right through the soul and spirit. It will discern truth from a lie, facts from fiction, reality from fantasy, spirit from carnality. Many believers are stuck year after year in fear,

God's Word is the
road map to a fulfilling life.

anxiety, condemnation, hopelessness, addiction, etc. because they continue to believe the lies repeating daily in their heads. These lies replay over and over like a stuck record player.

In our carnal, weak minds it is difficult to know whether the thought we just had was truth or a lie? That is why it is of the utmost importance to study God's Word as you embark on your journey of faith. It is the only way to ensure you are living in right believing.

You will continue to struggle and walk in defeat until the powerhouse controlling your life is not your mind, will, and emotions, but a strong, healthy spirit.

3. Be an example

God wants to use transformation in your life to prove to the world what is good and acceptable and perfect. The Bible tells us we are living epistles being read of all men (see 2 Corinthians 3:2). God longs to use your life as an example of grace and godliness to this hurting, lost world. His existence is fully demonstrated in the world when others behold His gracious transformation in you. Not everyone is reading his or her Bible, but you and I are read by everyone in our spheres of influence. Your life speaks messages to others. The question is: What message are you delivering? When your life reveals the true nature and character of Christ, His good and acceptable and perfect will is on display for the world to see.

It's amazing how far a bit of love and kindness really goes. Years ago, Holy Spirit impressed upon my heart to depart from every public interaction by declaring this blessing over their lives: "Have a blessed day!" Just this one small dose of kindness has brought encouragement, as well as love, to many strangers I might not otherwise have the opportunity to uplift. What I have noticed is that people witness the transformation of God in my life. They witness that my life is different. Transformation brought on by the renewal of the mind is clearly evident to those around us. 2 Corinthians 5:20 declares that we are ambassadors of Christ. God makes His appeal to the world through us. An ambassador is a representative. WOW! I am His representative! So are you. What sort of appeal is your life generating? You and I are the Body of Christ. We are His hands and feet to the world. We are the Bible others are reading. We must allow the Holy Spirit to transform our lives into what is good, acceptable, and the perfect will of God.

TESTIMONY

OK, I told you earlier that I would eventually get around to telling you how I overcame fear in my life. The first three years I was married, Steve worked the dayshift and because I had someone to sleep with every night, I rarely gave any thought to my fear. Until one day Steve was placed on the night shift and my fears were once again staring me in the face. My mind was suddenly filled with anxiety as I asked myself, *"What am I going to do now? I live in Chicago, seven hours away from my family. I have a child to take care of. Who is going to protect us while Steve is at work? How am I ever going to sleep again? Why are you doing this to me, Lord?"*

Our Father does not want His children to be hindered in any way. Freedom is God's desire for our lives. The appointed time for fear to be resolved in my life had come. It was time to mature. God wanted to show me whose I am. I knew 2 Timothy 1:7 declared, "God has not given us a spirit of fear," but then why was I still so afraid?

The first night Steve left for work I thought I would die. I left all of the lights on throughout the entire house, including the outside lights. I tuned the radio to my favorite Christian station and left it on all night. I numbly retreated to my room. Once again my childhood fears wrestled and fought to consume me. I wanted to cover my head. I wanted to pin the blinds. I lay still, as if I was petrified, but this time something was different. I had my heavenly Father to turn to. This time, the faithful Holy Spirit led me into prayer. I called out to my Father and divulged to Him how scared I really was. I asked Him to cover me, to cover my daughter, and to help me sleep.

I've never forgotten what happened next. It is as vivid today as it was that night twenty-three years ago. My faithful, heavenly Father spoke directly to my troubled heart through a vision. He showed me our house, viewed from the road on which it sat. The entire house was covered with the blood of Jesus. The blood flowed from the roof downward. Then, God allowed me to not only see, but to hear, the conversation Satan was having with his army. Satan was standing outside with a legion of demons armed and ready to harm me. I very clearly and distinctly heard him say, "Come on! We have to go on to the next house. This one is covered by the blood of Jesus."

Satan and his army left in disappointment and defeat. That moment changed my life forever. A mighty weight was lifted from me. God gave me the tools I needed to disarm the stronghold of fear that had been on my life since I was a child. I simply chose to replace my fears with the truth Holy Spirit had revealed to me. This is a choice I make every day. We give fear too much control and the way we do this is through our minds. Fear is nothing more than **F**alse **E**vidence **A**ppearing **R**eal.

I learned that night that my life and all that belonged to me was protected at all times by my heavenly Father. Psalm 121:3-4 tells us that our mighty God never sleeps nor slumbers. 2 Chronicles 16:9 became my strength: *"For the eyes of the Lord run to and fro throughout the whole earth, to shew himself strong in the behalf of them whose heart is perfect toward him."* By "perfect" the writer means perfectly aligned, loyal, and fully committed. That scared little girl is now a mighty warrior. Renewing my mind in Christ has become the power and strength of my life. *"In peace I will lie down and sleep, for you alone, Lord, make me dwell in safety"* (Psalm 4:8 NIV).

I would be lying if I said fear has never returned to taunt me, because it has, but I will never again give fear the power to control my life. My friend, God has you and everything that belongs to you in the palm of His hand. Whatever is troubling you, talk to your Father about it. And then, REST! Sleep like a baby, surrounded by the One who never sleeps.

"Do not be afraid of the terrors of the night, nor the arrow that flies in the day. Do not dread the disease that stalks in darkness, nor the disaster that strikes at midday. Though a thousand fall at your side, though ten thousand are dying around you, these evils will not touch you" (Psalm 91:5-7 NLT).

When dealing with the lusts of the flesh, the lusts of the eyes, the pride of life, and those lying emotions, bring every thought into captivity and release truth from God's word regarding these strongholds. How do you release truth? By thinking upon truth and declaring truth over your situation.

Philippians 4:8 proclaims: *"Finally, brothers and sisters, whatever is true, noble, right, pure, lovely, admirable–if anything is excellent or praise-worthy–think about such things."* The Apostle Paul understood the daily battle between the soul and spirit. He proclaimed in Romans 7:15, *"For what I want to do I do not do, but what I hate I do"* (NIV).

Dear reader, it is now time to take inventory. Are YOU out of your mind? Are you living by truth or living life according to what you think and how you feel? If you cannot truthfully respond that you are thinking with a renewed mind, then you have now been given the powerful tools to move forward in the process of renewing the mind. And, dear friend, it is a process! It can take years to train our carnal mindsets, but I dare you to walk each day using these tools you have been given. After all, you are only responsible for TODAY.

A healthy mind yields a healthy life!

Rhythm Reflections

1. What does the term "living sacrifice" mean to you?

2. Since putting your faith in Christ, has God asked you to give up specific things? What? How did His request make you feel? Do (or did) you see His request as "taking" from you?

3. Of the spirit, soul, and body which part is necessary for communion and worship with God? ______________________
Which of the three is controlling you? What can you do to strengthen your spirit?

4. Read 2 Corinthians 5:17 again. Jot down a few things that you have continued to struggle with since becoming a believer.

5. According to 2 Corinthians 10:3-6, what MUST you take captive?

6. In your own words, explain the difference between wisdom and knowledge.

7. List what Hebrews 4:12 has to say about the Word of God:

8. You are a living epistle, read by those people in your sphere of influence. Your life is delivering some kind of message. What message is your life currently displaying?

9. Brainstorm things you can begin to do today, great or small, that can make a huge impact.

10. If you feel you are in need of wisdom, where should you go?

11. Ask God to show you specifically the people in your life to whom He is calling you to be an ambassador for Him.

Prayer

Father, You purchased my life with the blood of Your Son Jesus and redeemed me so that I could walk in fellowship and partnership with You. I belong to You. I thank You that Your spirit lives inside of me, enabling me to walk in the fullness of victory. I desire to die to every part of my life that does not reflect Your thoughts and character. As I commit to becoming a student of Your Word, I ask You to fill me with all wisdom and truth that transforms my life and renews my carnal mind. May I become Your faithful ambassador to this lost and dark world. In Jesus' Name I pray. Amen.

Use the space below to write any specific prayer requests you have:

Chapter 5
Faith Speaks

"If ye abide in me, and my words abide in you, ye shall ask what ye will, and it shall be done unto you."

—John 15:7

Abide in Him

I PURPOSELY POSITIONED this chapter after the chapter on Renewing the Mind because these two principles work congruently. The word "abide" in the above scripture actually means "to take up residence." It does not mean "to visit on occasion!" When we take up intimate residence in Christ, we become saturated with truth and purpose. His will then becomes our will. Therefore, we can ask anything that we desire and it will be granted because our request is in alignment with His will.

Recognize His Voice

Because I abide in God's Word, I have learned to clearly recognize His voice. Are you aware of the number of voices speaking into your head on a daily basis? One reference shows that the human brain processes approximately 70,000 thoughts per day. The question is: Who is doing the talking? Is it a friend? Your boss? The enemy of your soul? It can even be YOU. All of these sources have the ability to speak into your life and influence you negatively or positively.

People mock the fact that God still speaks directly to us. Even those who call themselves Christians do this! I have personally encountered some who believe that God does not currently speak to

You learn to recognize Christ's voice by abiding in Him.

His people and that the Bible is our only source of communication from God. They believe that we still have the privilege of speaking to Him in prayer, but somehow do not believe that He still speaks to us.

Years ago, I was invited to a meeting with a youth pastor at one of the local churches in the town we lived in at the time. I quickly realized after my arrival that he had extended the invitation to me with a definite agenda in mind. He wanted to pick my brain, dissect my beliefs, and usurp his earthly authority over me as a man. As I sat in his presence, he commanded me not to speak. I was told that as a woman I had no right to speak.

Then he proceeded to ask me a series of questions beginning with this one. "So, I hear you talk to God?"

Bewildered, I responded with, "Yes, I talk with God every day."

He replied, "But, does He speak to you?"

"Of course He speaks to me," I answered.

In his self-righteous conceit he said, "Well, when are you going to write a book and tell the rest of US what God is saying?"

I was shocked. The Bible tells us plainly: *"My sheep hear my voice, and I know them, and they follow me"* (John 10:27). How hard is that to understand? Jesus spoke those words. "My sheep HEAR my voice. . ."

Walking in relationship with Jesus really is simple, my friends. We are the ones who have made it so very complicated with our many interpretations. God speaks to us through His Word. He speaks to us through the office of pastor, evangelist, teacher, apostle, and prophet. God speaks to us through songs. He speaks to us through His still small voice in our conscience. God can use *anything* He desires to speak a message to us: nature, signs, children, and dreams, to name a few. God could even choose to speak to us through animals if He wanted to, as He did in Numbers 22:28. He is a God who still speaks to His children and because He still speaks, we must learn to listen.

Recognizing God's voice will assist you in filtering out all the other voices speaking in your head. You will learn to recognize God's voice as you linger in His Presence. I know it's difficult and unheard of nowadays, in a world of fast-paced living, but we need to actually discipline ourselves to be still before God. We need to learn how to be quiet before God. Prayer is communication between you and God. That means there is a time to talk and there is a time to listen. Have you ever had a friend who does ALL the talking and you can never get a word in edgewise? That friend is selfish and only thinks about his or her needs and desires. They rarely stop to listen and care about any needs or exciting news you may have.

If we're honest with ourselves, this is often how we approach our God. "Father, will you...? Can I...? I need..." I can see the lists now that we bring before God, our petitions and our requests. Dear friend, this is only a part of the pleasure you have of communicating with God. He is your Friend, but when does He get a chance to tell you His desires and His plans?

Lingering in His presence affords you the gift of beautiful friendship with your God and your Maker, the lover of your soul. Soon, you will find that your Friend also desires to speak to you. He longs to commune with you, just as He did in the Garden of Eden with Adam and Eve. There, He would come down in the cool of each day to commune with His creation. His desire to fellowship with us has not changed.

Often, we seek to impress God with great works or our many acts of service and while this is a part of our journey with God, it is not the most important or necessary part.

Reflect on the story of Mary and Martha found in Luke 10:38-42:

"As Jesus and his disciples were on their way, he came to a village where a woman named Martha opened her home to him. She had a sister called Mary, who sat at the Lord's feet listening to what he said. But Martha was distracted by all the preparations that had to be made. She came to him and asked, 'Lord, don't you care that my sister has left me to do the work by myself? Tell her to help me!'

"'Martha, Martha,' the Lord answered, 'you are worried and upset about many things, but few things are needed–or indeed only one. Mary has chosen what is better, and it will not be taken away from her.'"

Here, we see Martha busy with acts of service unto Jesus.

Having Jesus visit her private home had to be nerve-racking. Personally, I think it was mindful of Martha to show hospitality toward her special guest. She wanted everything to be just right. Cleaning the house, preparing a wonderful meal, and serving Jesus was important to Martha. Notice, in the text that Jesus did not say the acts of Martha were not beneficial or important. He only said that Mary had chosen the *better* part at that time. Not one of us would be any use to society or to the kingdom if all we ever did was sit at the feet of Jesus. He desires for action to accommodate our faith. However, you have to enter into a balanced relationship between acts of service and intimacy with Jesus. Notice also in the story that Mary was not sitting at the feet of Jesus talking. The passage says she was listening.

If you really want to see results from your faith, get in agreement with God's plan and His desires for your life. By listening to His still small voice and reading His Word, your petitions, requests, and declarations will begin to line up with His will for your life. When you learn to speak according to His will, you will see results every time.

Declare His Promises

Let me be very real with you. At times, I do not know if what I desire in my heart lines up with the will of God or not. When I encounter this kind of situation, I simply present my request to God and ask Him to be Lord over my request. I ask Him to perform His will over the matter.

Sometimes, the answer to my request is, "No." I have learned to be OK with this. This is part of living a surrendered life to my heavenly Father. I have learned that if He tells me no, it is only because He has a better plan to bless me. Do not be disappointed that your good plan was given a no. Get excited that His GREAT plan is on its way if you will remain surrendered to His authority and joyful in trust.

Sometimes, God tells me to, "Wait!" No one enjoys waiting and I am certainly no exception. However, I can promise you that every time He tells me to wait, I am rewarded in time with something greater than I ever imagined or requested. We serve a loving, faithful, generous God who enjoys blessing His children with every good thing. Learn to visualize God sitting on your couch, pleased for you to sit alongside Him or even cuddle up in His lap. Stop seeing God as the untouchable master of the universe and gaze upon Him as the God of YOUR universe. He is not some vast God, high above the heavens, who cannot be bothered or reached. He is a God who is concerned with the details of your day. He knows everything about you and your life. So, approach Him with confidence (see Hebrews 4:15-16). He awaits your attention, your touch, and your adoration. Know that He desires for you to sit close; He's waiting to commune with you. It is the very reason you were created.

Before we can decree or speak forth a promise from God, we must first learn to see the promise as ours through the eyes of faith. God told Abraham in Genesis 13:14-15 (NIV): *"The Lord said to Abram after Lot had parted from him, 'Look around from where you are, to the north and south, to the east and west. All the land that you see I will give to you and your offspring forever.'"*

In human reality, the truth was that Abraham did not even have a single descendant born unto him at the time this promise was given. Still, as Abraham BELIEVED and DECLARED the promise of the Lord with his mouth, the promise was activated in the earthly realm by the Holy Spirit. In my walk with God, I have learned to accept the unseen promises of my Lord as my "new reality." It matters not what I hear or see in the earth. When my God tells me something, it is done! (see Acts 27:25) My part is to believe and to partner with God in bringing the promise to pass through the declaration of faith. This process will always involve the words of your mouth. I love what Job 22:28 teaches us: *"Thou shalt decree a thing, and it shall be established unto thee: and the light shall shine upon thy ways."*

As you begin to operate by this principle, it is important to note that this verse is not teaching us how to develop a "name it and claim it" strategy. There is much teaching in the Body of Christ that we can have whatever we name and claim. Contrary to this belief, I have not found that I can claim to have a Cadillac and awaken to it the next morning, sitting in my driveway. What I have found to be stable and true is the fact that when God speaks His desire for my life into my spirit, as I believe His words and activate the power of manifestation through declaration, in time I always see fulfillment of the promise. This is what Job is referring to.

Both life and death are in the power of YOUR tongue (see Proverbs 18:21). It matters greatly what you choose to say. You have the power to decree either victory or defeat with the words that you speak. When you choose to declare over and over that "nothing good ever happens to you" or that "things will never get any better in your life," you give power to the atmosphere of defeat. However, as you train your mouth to say things such as: "I am the righteousness of God in Christ Jesus and His blessings chase me down every day" or "God is working all things together for my good," these statements create the kind of atmosphere necessary for victorious living. Be conscious of the words coming out of your mouth. Most of the time, many of the phrases we speak repeatedly are nothing more than bad habits we have developed. We do not even realize what we are actually saying. But, from this day forward, you need to become of aware of the words coming forth from your mouth and discipline your tongue to speak forth life.

In the 3rd chapter of James, we learn that our tongue is the smallest member of our body, but as the tongue goes, so does our entire life. James references the fact that in order to control the entire body of a horse, all that is needed is to place a small bit between the teeth of the horse and the animal will proceed in any direction in which the bit is pulled.

Ships are guided in a likewise way. Our family loves to go on cruises. We have been on the largest cruise ships in the world. It blew our minds to realize that the entire huge ship was directionally controlled by a small rudder. Friend, as your tongue goes, so does your entire life. That is why it is so very important to be aware of your speech. You are actually determining the course of your life by the words that you speak. Learn to partner together with God through your speech. Declaration that is in agreement with God is essential if you ever expect to see the things you are believing for manifested in your life.

"It is written: 'I believed, therefore, I have spoken.' Since we have the same spirit of faith, we also believe and therefore speak" (2 Corinthians 4:13 NIV).

TESTIMONY

I was sitting at the baseball park on a Saturday afternoon in 2005, watching my son play in his Little League Baseball game. I was minding my own business, simply enjoying the beautiful day. Suddenly, I heard the Holy Spirit say to me, "You're going to be building a house soon." I thought to myself, *WHAT??* Now, I had not even asked God to let me build a house, but what I did do was walk away from a house I really wanted one year ago to that very month. The reason I walked away was because God had spoken to my spirit that it was not the house for me and that I needed to let it go. I did so joyfully, but disappointed. The house was built on 5 acres and, even though it needed a lot of work, I really, really wanted us to buy it.

After clearly hearing the voice of the Holy Spirit at the ball park, I was excited to return home and share the news with Steve. Instead of joyfully responding, Steve rebuked me, while adding that I was always wanting a new house and I was never satisfied. He reminded me of the beautiful house we already lived in. My heart was broken. It was not that I wasn't happy with my current home. Geez, I hadn't even asked to build this new house. I was simply conveying the message I clearly heard from the Spirit. When I sought the Lord about Steve's response, He simply told me to be still and be quiet. So, I obeyed.

One week later, Steve asked me if I wanted to go golfing with him. I do not golf, but I love to ride in the cart with him and enjoy the peaceful serenity and time alone together. Toward the end of the course, while Steve prepared to tee off, the Holy Spirit came upon me once again and said, "You're going to be building a house soon."

I looked at Steve and said, "Honey, we are going to be building a house soon."

He looked at me and said, "I know." You see, God had been dealing with him, too.

We decided that we did not want to build in a subdivision. We'd had our eye on a few acre lots close to my mom and dad's house for twelve years, but we didn't even know who owned them. It had only been a dream in our hearts. My mother drove to the county courthouse, seeking the name of the owner of the lots. Surprisingly, she found that out of the six acre lots that were available, five of them were owned by a man that lived a few houses down from her and one of the lots, which happened to be right smack dab in the middle of the whole plat, was owned by the Madison Church of Christ.

Mom corresponded with her close neighbor who owned five of the lots and was informed that he was not interested in selling. Next, she called the Madison Church of Christ. The pastor informed my mom that he had called a special board meeting the night before to vote on whether or not to sell the lot. The board had decided that night to sell this particular lot for $22,000. At that time in the Nashville area, acre lots were going for $50-60,000 an acre.

Unbelievably enough, this lot was also directly across the street from Old Hickory Lake. Mom was the first caller. Without even thinking about it, she responded to the man, "We'll take it!"

Steve followed up with several conversations over the next few days and we entered into a contract with the church to purchase the lot contingent upon the property perking for a septic system. We were so excited! We knew God was making a way for us to live on one of these lots in a miraculous way. The city took several soil samples from the property and determined that our lot would not accommodate a septic system. I knew in my spirit that God had chosen this property for us. I had exercised my faith and stepped out in obedience to begin the building process God had spoken into my spirit, but this news crushed me. I was so disappointed, my heart was in my stomach.

I had to get off to myself and allow the news to process. Once I stepped away from the noise, I heard God say to me, "Do not accept this news! This land belongs to you. Walk the property just as the children of Jericho did. Make seven laps around the perimeter of the property without speaking a word. On the seventh lap, I want you to shout a shout of victory. Then, pour anointing oil inside every hole the city dug for a soil sample."

A sense of excitement returned in me. I didn't know how, but I knew somehow everything was going to be alright. The next day I called the city soil supervisor to schedule a second test, with hopes of a different result. The cranky old man denied my request. A few days later, the Holy Spirit led me to the county courthouse. I pulled the surveyed dimensions on all six acres. A lady on staff asked if she might help me with anything. I explained our situation to her. I told her that we really desired to live on this particular lot, but the city had denied us a septic system.

She checked the specifications on the lot herself and returned to me with astonishing news. She said, "Did you know this lot is what we call a 'grandfather lot'?"

"No," I replied, "what does that mean?"

She said, "It means that years and years ago when the city zoned this piece of property, a clause was attached to it declaring that the city could not deny anyone the right to build on this property regardless of soil test results."

I could hardly believe what I was hearing! This meant that we COULD live on this property. This meant that no one could deny us access to build, just as God had spoken to me. I returned home to share the new information with Steve.

Within a couple weeks, we signed the documents and closed the sale of our property. We were even able to pay cash

for the land. Suddenly, fear tried to spring up in my spirit. Yes, this land had been 'grandfathered' and yes, we were given permission to purchase and build, but what if the soil really wouldn't accommodate a septic system? What if we built our dream home, but constantly had problems with the septic system? What a disaster this could have been!

Once again, I had to get alone with my God and listen to His still small voice. I heard Him say, "This property has been yours from the beginning. Even before you were born, I zoned this exact lot with a 'grandfather' clause so that nothing could inhibit you building here. I am your GRAND FATHER!"

That was 2005. We moved into our new home on September 3, 2006. It was everything we had ever dreamed of and we never had a single issue with the septic system!

1. Abide in Him. Listen to His voice. Declare His promises. As you reflect on these steps toward building your faith, which of these areas are you doing well? Which do you need to work on?

2. The human brain has around 70,000 thoughts each day. What is the source of most of your thinking? What unhealthy thoughts do you need to get rid of? Which healthy thoughts can you increase?

3. Write about the various ways God speaks to you. Be specific.

4. A faith-filled life is a balance between acts of service and listening. List ways that you might be so busy "doing" at the expense of "listening." Where in your schedule can you intentionally set aside time to listen?

5. If someone were to say to you, “God doesn’t speak to people anymore,” how would you respond?

6. Many do not trouble God with the details about their lives because they believe He is too busy to worry about such things. Does this thinking affect how you view God? Do you see Him more as a God who is big and unapproachable or as a God who invites you to sit on His lap?

7. How important is the step of “declaration” in the faith process?

8. “As the tongue goes, so does your life.” What does this statement mean to you? How have you seen this truth put into action?

9. In what ways do you need to discipline your tongue in order to make a change in your life direction?

10. In the testimony shared beginning on page 82, I explained how I needed to have faith in a promise from God, even when circumstances pointed to a different outcome. Share a time when you heard from God and had to hold tightly to His word, even though you didn’t know how it would all work out.

(Space to continue question 10)

Prayer

Daddy God, I love that You not only know my name, but You are acquainted with every detail of my life. Yes, You are indeed the God of the entire Universe, but You are also the God of my personal universe and You desire to communicate with me. You love when I bring my prayers and petitions before You, but You also experience my love for You when I stop to listen to what You have to say back to me. Reveal Your will to me, Daddy. I want to know what You think about. What are Your desires? What do You desire to tell me? I repent for the times I was too busy to hear. Grant me the enabling grace to abide, listen, and declare. I desire to experience Your will for my life and fulfill Your kingdom here on earth. In Jesus' Name I pray. Amen.

Use the space below to write any specific prayer requests you have:

Chapter 6

Overcoming the Orphan Mentality

"For you created my inmost being, you knit me together in my mother's womb. I praise you because I am fearfully and wonderfully made; your works are wonderful. I know that full well. My frame was not hidden from you when I was made in the secret place. When I was woven together in the depths of the earth, your eyes saw my unformed body. All the days ordained for me were written in your book before one of them came to pass."

–Psalm 139:13-16

A STORY WAS once told of an eaglet who fell from his nest and was separated from his family. A mother hen took pity on the eaglet and raised it as her own. As it grew, the eaglet pecked and shuffled along the ground with the other sibling chicks, never realizing that life could be any different. Until one day, it looked up and saw another eagle, soaring high in the sky and it marveled.

So often in life, we are that eaglet. Life's circumstances, wounds, bad choices, and environments keep us separated from God, who is the very source of our identity. We peck around and shuffle along to the beat of our familiar surroundings. We adopt the behaviors and mindsets of our environment. Whether healthy or unhealthy, godly or ungodly, these outside influences contribute toward shaping the mindset by which we conduct our lives. The eaglet was raised and surrounded by chicks. Therefore, he walked around likewise; imitating and limiting himself by pecking his way through life as if he, too, were a common chicken. Yes, he was doing alright and yes, he was surviving, but the problem was that he was born an eagle, created by God to SOAR!

When I look back over my life, I determine that I was only halfway living before I met Jesus. Being only half a person, I lived the best way I knew how and tried to make good decisions, but I did not really even know who I was. I had no real sense of purpose and was void of healthy identity. I lived as if I were a spiritual orphan.

I believe every person who has not accepted God's invitation as loving Father lives with limitation–as only half the person they were created to become–because our true identity is always found within a personal relationship with God our Creator.

Read the verse which led off this chapter. Psalm 139 speaks beautiful affirmation to our hearts, reminding us Who created us. Our identity is found in the One who created us. It is solidified in the One who died for us. We enter into this world through sin, but we are not destined to remain there. Through the sacrificial death of Jesus Christ, and most importantly through His victorious resurrection, we have been offered the opportunity to become adopted sons and daughters of the Most High God.

*"For God previously ordained us (destined us) to be adopted as His own children through Jesus Christ, in accordance with the purpose of His will [because it pleased Him and was His kind intent]" (*Ephesians 1:5 Amplified Bible).

When you accept Jesus Christ as your personal savior and surrender your life to Him as Master, you become born-again; fresh and anew, sealed with the Holy Spirit of promise. You are no longer an orphan, left alone to decipher your way through life, but you are a son or daughter of God. This position carries with it great benefits.

"Praise the Lord, my soul, and forget not all his benefits–who forgives all your sins and heals all your diseases, who redeems your life from the pit and crowns you with love and compassion, who satisfies your desires with good things so that your youth is renewed like the eagle's" (Psalm 103:2-5 NIV).

As sons and daughters of God, we become heirs of God and co-heirs with Christ. When God raised His Son from the dead, He positioned Him in the highest place of authority to reign forever. God seated His Son in the heavens at His own right hand, far above all principality, power, might, dominion, and every name that is named, not only in this world, but also in the world to come. All things have been placed under our Savior's feet. Because Jesus Christ lives within us, we too have been given this same inheritance.

Why then, do we succumb to mediocrity? Why are we living beneath our spiritual privileges? I believe our own ignorance of biblical truths hinders us from living victoriously and greatly aids in the development of an orphan mindset. It is possible to be a Christian and yet live as an orphan!

The Fatherless Generation

Orphans are displaced and often feel unloved or unaccepted. I have encountered many in the Body of Christ who, despite being born-again, still feel personally unloved, unaccepted, and unworthy of their position in Christ. They are spiritual orphans. Those with this unhealthy spiritual condition have a disconnect between knowing God is their Father and accepting that they truly are one of His children and that He loves them unconditionally. Intellectually you may comprehend God as Father, but emotionally do not feel His acceptance and love on a personal, individual basis. This spiritual condition is common among believers who lack a healthy, godly identity that provides justification of one's worth and value as God's child. Friend, this orphan mentality steals your inheritance!

The current generation of children in America is sadly referred to as the "Fatherless Generation." They are a generation of thousands living without the presence, influence, and love of an earthly, biological father. I was shocked to learn that the lack of an earthly father or the lack of a "good" earthly father present in one's life lends to overwhelming emotional and physical problems.

I want to share some enlightening statistics:

- 43% of US children live without their father [US Dept. of Census]
- 90% of homeless and runaway children are from fatherless

Ignorance of biblical truth hinders victorious living.

homes [US D.H.H.S., Bureau of the Census]
- 80% of rapists motivated by displaced anger come from fatherless homes [Criminal Justice & Behavior, Vol.14, pp.403-26, 1978]
- 71% of pregnant teens lack a father [US Dept. of Health and Human Services press release, Friday, March 26, 1999]
- 63% of youth suicides are from fatherless homes [US D.H.H.S., Bureau of the Census]
- 85% of children who exhibit behavioral disorders come from fatherless homes [Center For Disease Control]

A father has the ability to speak identity into your life. A father gives you your name! In Genesis, we see that God gave Adam (the first father) the important job of naming all the animals. God said to Adam, "Whatever YOU call them, it shall be." Fathers have that ability to name you. Not only do we take on the surname of our earthly fathers when we are born, but a father also has the ability to speak identity into your soul. Therefore, the role of a father is important for the healthy development of one's soul. He has the power to speak life into the soul of a child or speak the crushing blows of death. When you have not had the privilege of a godly, moral, loving earthly father present in your life, speaking identity and truth into your spirit, you are more apt to suffer from identity crisis. Sometimes, we are not even aware of the crisis. We shuffle through life just like the eaglet did, doing the very best we can with what we have been given in the environment surrounding us, but we are operating from a place of limitation and often brokenness.

I shared with you in a previous chapter that I became pregnant at seventeen years of age. To be honest with you, I knew premarital sex was wrong. I knew I shouldn't participate in such acts, but I did not know who I was. My parents had divorced when I was only five years old and my dad removed himself from our home. Mom remarried a wonderful man when I was nine. Both of my dads loved, cared for, and supported me, but neither of them spoke spiritual truth into my life. Neither father spoke true identity into my spirit. Therefore, I operated from a spiritual deficit.

Just as not having an earthly father can bankrupt a person's emotions, causing erratic behavior and the inability to exercise healthy judgment, so will living as a spiritual orphan.

The orphan mentality has caused many in the Body of Christ to accept the lies of the enemy.

- I am in God's family, but I am not as good as so and so.
- I am in God's family, but I am not as spiritual as so and so.
- Because I messed up yesterday, or last month, or last year, I am not worthy to ask God for anything.
- I know I am a child of God, but I'm not one of His CHOSEN kids.
- I am all alone.
- I am stuck and I always will be.
- Nothing good ever happens to me.
- My life sucks.
- No one will ever really love me.
- I will always be sick.
- I can never do anything right.

These are just a few unhealthy examples of the orphan mentality. When we view ourselves any less than the way God sees us, we operate from an orphan identity. Proverbs 23:7 (Amplified) reminds us, *"For as he thinks in his heart, so is he."* In other words, the way you truly feel about yourself sets the course for your life. That is why it is of the utmost importance to feed your spirit with the truths of God's Word. Only when your spirit is nourished and healthy can you live in balance and truth. Christ offered Himself as the perfect sacrifice and was powerfully resurrected so that you would have nothing missing and nothing broken in your life. In Him, you find the fullness of truth and grace and there is never an excuse to lack spiritually, emotionally, or physically. His provisions encompass your needs.

How long will you allow the hurts and disappointments you've experienced in the past to become an idol in your life? When you would rather hold on to past hurts and anger rather than allow God to heal your soul, then you have created an idol of your pain. I have prayed with many hurting people who God graciously desired to heal, only to find them resistant to His offer. Many desire to hold on to their hurtful past experiences because it gives them an excuse to remain bitter, offended, and emotionally handicapped. I know this sounds absurd, but it's true. You can only use your pitiful past and your victim's mentality as your life's message and excuse for so long. Otherwise, you void the transformational, healing power of the cross. Let it go. Allow the Father to heal your mind, fill you with peace, and resurrect your life with a fresh, healthy identity.

What a privilege it is for a child to grow up in a home where the father affirms, loves, and guides his children to emotional wholeness and healthy life. I am blessed to have the kind of husband who guides our children by example, love, moral principles, and biblical truth. This loving guidance has afforded them both security and stability. They certainly haven't navigated through life free from challenges, but with each challenging season, the foundational identity formed within each of them by both their earthly father and their heavenly Father has kept them sure and steadfast. They do not question who they are nor whose they are. Our love and the love of God remain constant in their lives. The power that resides within them constantly speaks to their spirit, reminding them that they are the head and not the tail and that they can and will do all things with excellence through Christ who gives them strength.

You may be reading this chapter and thinking, "I wish I had a father like that." Unfortunately, in life, we are not afforded the privilege of choosing our parents. Maybe you grew up with a father who did not encourage you, who never spoke the words, "I love you," or never provided a father's deep acceptance and affection. The absence of a strong earthly father will cause you to make preconceived assumptions about your heavenly Father who loves you so much. However, the two cannot be compared. You cannot control the choices of your earthly father. But you can control your own choice to accept Father God's personal invitation to become His son or daughter. Your heavenly Father gave His only begotten Son so that YOU could be forgiven of your sinful past and be ransomed by His great love. He is a father who loves you unconditionally and awaits your homecoming. You are safe inside His arms of love. He waits to fill you with power and purpose and promises to never leave you nor forsake you.

Your New Name

When I turned eighteen, I met my heavenly Father and the way I saw myself quickly began to change. As I poured God's Word into my heart, His affections and purpose for me began to mirror the way I viewed my life. I began to realize that my life mattered and that I was a valuable part of His family. In order to stop the cycle of the orphan mentality, you and I must become aware of our true identity in Christ. It is important that you learn to rest in the grace of God. Grace is the unearned, undeserved favor of God that rests upon all of His children simply because of our position in Christ. You cannot earn grace. You cannot purchase grace. Grace does not decrease when you make a mistake, nor does it increase when you operate on your best behavior. God's grace over you is constant. There is no respect of persons with God. He doesn't love one of us more than another. You are His child and you already have His approval. You do not need to earn it. Stop looking to another person, another drug, material possessions, or your career to fulfill you spiritually, emotionally, and physically. Allow your Father to bring you into wholeness. He is a friend that sticks closer than any brother and He desires to turn your mourning into dancing, your tears into laughter, and your brokenness into beauty.

By His grace, God desires to give you a new name. Accept it! He desires to speak His new name for you into your spirit. In all of your heartache and brokenness, He longs to reveal to you who you really are and fill your life with purpose. In 1998, I was lovingly given a new name by my heavenly Father. He awakened me in the early morning hours and spoke to me, saying, "You shall be called the 'Repairer of the Breach.'" The message was very clear, although I had no idea what it meant, nor had I ever heard mention of this phrase before. Weeks later, I was reading a book by Joyce Meyer. In it, she referenced "Repairer of the Breach" from Isaiah 58. Quickly, I turned to this chapter in the Bible and I, too, was given a spiritual awakening. There, defined in the verses of Isaiah 58:6-12, was MY new name, new identity, and new purpose. Since this monumental day in my life, I have been partnering with God to accept my new name and assignment. I have allowed His truths to mold my identity and reshape my mindset. In Christ, I am everything my heavenly Father says that I am! Today, I do not operate from a spiritual deficit, but from a healthy storehouse of truth, power, and authority.

You may say, "What's in a name?" Your name assigns purpose and identity. When God changed a person's name, He was actually changing their identity. He was saying, "From this day forward, you are no longer the person you used to be. You have been given a new name, new identity, and new purpose."

Many times in the Bible, we find men and women who received a new name from God. For instance, Saul met Jesus on the road to Damascus. He had spent his entire life upholding the laws as a Pharisee, convicting and executing Christians. But when his spiritual eyes were awakened by Jesus, he was given new identity, direction, and purpose. "Your name shall no longer be Saul, but Paul the Apostle." We read also that Jacob's name was changed to Israel, Abram's name was changed to Abraham, Sarai's name was changed to Sarah, and Simon Bar-Jonah's name was changed to Peter.

Even as you allow God to change your name and identity, there will always be those familiar with your past who will choose to refer to you as the old person. They do this because they cannot comprehend the miraculous transformation your life has undergone. We see examples of this from the life of Jesus. As Jesus began to step out in public ministry and perform miracles before the people's eyes, there were those who would not believe because for years they had played in the streets with this little boy. They knew His parents, Mary and Joseph, to be common people. Instead of comprehending the power and authority Jesus carried, He was reduced to remain the son of Joseph the carpenter (John 6:42). Awareness of this fact will afford you strength as you encounter others who insist on reminding you of your past and your many mistakes.

The information provided in this chapter is such an integral piece in the process of faith. Turn back and read once again the quick

God wants to awaken you to your true identity and destiny.

story of the displaced eaglet on page 91. Take note that the eaglet had fallen out of its nest and because he was isolated and rejected, he found acceptance and community among the first to embrace him—the chickens. However, his sphere of influence limited him from reaching his full potential and purpose. One day, as he peered high into the sky, the eaglet took note of a majestic eagle soaring above. With wings fully spread across the sky, the eaglet was suddenly awakened to new freedom and purpose he had never encountered before. His day of awakening had arrived.

Is this such a day for you? It is not by chance that you are reading this book. No matter what your reason for purchasing it, God has another plan. A plan to awaken you to your true identity and destiny. The journey will require that you walk by faith. It may also require that you make a change in the company of friends you currently keep. You see, as long as the eaglet associated himself with the chickens, he remained ignorant and uninspired of his true destiny. In order to reach his full potential, the eaglet had to make a decision to leave the chickens and fly among the other eagles. If you dream of a better life and you know you were created to do more than you are currently accomplishing, then it will be necessary to surround yourself with like-minded individuals—people who no longer live as orphans, but saturate their minds with powerful, inspiring biblical truths. Begin to create a circle of friends who speak life-giving identity into your soul. Consider joining a church, a youth group, a men's or women's Bible study, a Sunday School class, or accept a godly mentor into your life. Iron sharpens iron—so shall we sharpen one another. Take the first step today toward becoming all that you were created by God to be!

 TESTIMONY

When I became pregnant at age seventeen, Steve and I were inexperienced, unsaved, unaware kids. Both of us had been raised in broken homes. Even though I didn't agree with abortion, my first thought was to abort the child and move forward unashamedly. I was filled with dread at the thought of telling my mother. She had no idea I wasn't a virgin. Steve encouraged me to have the baby and join him in marriage. Two months later, on September 10, 1988, we stood before family and friends and innocently pledged our love and commitment to each other. Our lives suddenly and drastically changed. Steve went from being a heroic athlete with little to no responsibility to being a husband, provider, and father. I was a senior in high school, with my entire senior year to complete before graduation. I quickly digressed from being a well-liked, popular student to the class of 1989's object of scorn. Lost and alone, I walked the halls of Mt. Juliet High School, feeling like I had a large letter "A" on the left side of my chest.

We didn't have a thing to our name! Steve took a job at a nearby sign company making around five dollars an hour. In the evenings I waited tables at Cracker Barrel. My mom and step-dad purchased a new home complete with a downstairs apartment so that we might somehow feel like we had a place of our own.

Following my senior year, I met my savior, Jesus Christ. He transformed my life. Though my past was marred with wrong decisions and an unhealthy identity, God redeemed me. He salvaged my life and my purpose. He purchased my sin and in exchange I was given life abundantly: Abundant grace enabling me with wisdom to become a godly wife and mother, abundant forgiveness that allowed me to stand in purity before His throne, and abundant mercy so that I never needed to walk in shame again. Through His Spirit, I was provided ears to hear and a heart to understand His truths.

My husband surrendered his life to the Lord as well and was graciously transformed into a loving, giving husband and father. He is the hardest-working man I know, selflessly giving to his family on a daily basis. He is a man of great moral character. God has made him to be successful in all he puts his hands to. Even though neither of us had the opportunity to go to college, God has blessed our lives in stature and prosperity as if we did.

At the writing of this book, we have been faithfully and joyfully married for twenty-seven years. Like Christ, we have become givers. Givers not only to our children, family, church, and community, but God has enlarged our territory of influence around the world. Two broken children, who were clueless and living as orphans, are now used by God to influence godly marriage and families. Two 'broke as a joke' kids are now used by God to assist people around the world in financial need. The young girl and boy who were abruptly thrown into parenting have now successfully raised two beautiful, God-fearing, moral, intelligent, compassionate contributors to society, who are focused on the needs of others. Alyse and Bryce both have successful careers that allow them to live independently from us as parents, and graciously partner with us in family ministry at Repairing the Breach Ministries, Inc. Most importantly, through digesting the truths of the Bible and speaking life into the lives of our children, we have successfully stopped the generational orphan mindset from controlling our family any longer.

Humbly, I offer all the praise, honor, and glory to God!

1. Before I accepted Jesus Christ into my life, I was only halfway living. Since giving my life to Him, I have never felt displaced, alone, or unaccepted. Have you made a personal commitment to Him yet? If so, please write down the things you remember from your decision to accept Christ. If you have not, you can right now. Turn to page 156 of this book and allow me to guide you through the steps of salvation.

2. Proverbs 23:7 reads, "As a man thinks in his heart, so is he." How you truly feel about yourself sets the course for your life. What healthy or unhealthy thoughts have directed a pattern or course in your life?

3. Can you identify with the orphan mentality described in this chapter?

4. What kind of earthly father do you have? In what ways has he contributed to your identity?

5. What mistakes or choices have you made in the past that you can now, looking back, attribute to a lack of a healthy, godly identity?

6. In what ways has your identity changed since accepting Jesus as your savior and taking on the name "Christian"?

7. Do you sense God assigning you a new name? What is it?

8. Think about your circle of friends and the company you keep. Do you need to make a change in the quantity or quality of time you spend with other people?

9. Share a testimony with your friend or someone in your study group as to how God has changed your life for the better.

Prayer

Father, Your Word teaches me in John 14:18 that You have not left me as an orphan in this world. You have given me Your Holy Spirit to comfort, guide, and teach me on a daily basis. You are a GRAND Father. Thank You for loving me and saving my soul. I ask You to fill me with the fullness of Your identity that equips me to carry out my purpose in Your kingdom. Help me to never again live beneath my privileges as Your child. I want to experience everything that Jesus died and rose again to provide me. Come, Lord Jesus, Come. I invite You into every area of my life to make any change You find necessary. May my life become a sweet fragrance unto You. In Jesus' Name I pray. Amen.

Use the space below to write any specific prayer requests you have:

Chapter 7
The Stumbling Blocks of Faith

"You were doing so well. Who **(or what)** *stopped you from being influenced by the truth? The arguments of the person* **(or thoughts)** *influencing you do not come from the One who is calling you."*
–Galatians 5:7-8 (my emphasis)

IN THIS CHAPTER we will explore three different stumbling blocks that ultimately impede the process of intimate faith. A stumbling block, by definition, is something that causes difficulty or hesitation in completing a task or moving forward. Sometimes, the obstacle blocking forward motion can be a physical one–such as a traffic jam, a physical ailment, or a sudden closed door. However, as we set out to cultivate a lifestyle of faith, I have found the stumbling block to most often stem from either a mental or spiritual hindrance–for instance, a thought that begins to attack and question the process of faith in your mind or simply a lack of spiritual knowledge, yielding ill-equipped tools for successful navigation of the course.

We often begin the process of faith with ease. It isn't until one or more of these opposing obstacles rears its ugly head that we have difficulty steadily maintaining the course of faith. As we progress through this chapter, ask Holy Spirit to reveal any of these three stumbling blocks presently at work within your spiritual walk.

1. Unbelief

Personal Unbelief

I believe it's easy enough to understand that if you are operating from a position of unbelief, the promises of God will not be able to manifest in your personal life.

Unbelief works in direct opposition to the supernatural act of faith. Unbelief peers through the lens of tangible evidence and dares not to succumb to false hope. Because real faith is the substance of things we cannot see, many who do not see first will not believe. I understand it can be somewhat difficult to receive the promises of God through the eyes of our own understanding, but that is why it is called faith. Faith can only be grasped through our spiritual senses. It is a supernatural act.

In John 20:19-29 (NIV), we are given a perfect example of the unbelief at work in the life of Thomas–one of the disciples of Jesus Christ:

"On the evening of that first day of the week, when the disciples were together, with the doors locked for fear of the Jewish leaders, Jesus came and stood among them and said, 'Peace be with you!' After he said this, he showed them his hands and side. The disciples were overjoyed when they saw the Lord.

"Again Jesus said, 'Peace be with you! As the Father has sent me, I am sending you.' And with that he breathed on them and said, 'Receive the Holy Spirit. If you forgive anyone's sins, their sins are forgiven; if you do not forgive them, they are not forgiven.'

"Now Thomas, one of the Twelve, was not with the disciples when Jesus came. So the other disciples told him, 'We have seen the Lord!'

"But he said to them, 'Unless I see the nail marks in his hands and put my finger where the nails were, and put my hand into his side, I will not believe.'

"A week later his disciples were in the house again, and Thomas was with them. Though the doors were locked, Jesus came and stood among them and said, 'Peace be with you!' Then he said to Thomas, 'Put your finger here; see my hands. Reach out your hand and put it into my side. Stop doubting and only believe.'

"Thomas said to him, 'My Lord and my God!'

"Then Jesus told him, 'Because you have seen me, you have believed; blessed are those who have not seen and yet have believed.'"

Thomas exemplified the classic symptom of unbelief: "I will not believe until I see tangible evidence to support my hopes."

In this process of faith, rarely will there be any tangible evidence to support your act of faith. Usually the promises and desires God asks us to believe for will go directly against all human reasoning, ability, and expectation.

God promised Abraham (Genesis 18) that Sarah would bear him a child in her old age. Now, Sarah was not simply old, but the Bible tells us that she was also beyond her child-bearing years. I translate that to mean that Sarah had already passed through menopause. We also read that Abraham was no spring chicken himself. Defying all odds, as our God loves to do, He spoke the promise to Abraham saying, "This time next year your wife will bear you a son." When Sarah heard the spoken word, she laughed, exclaiming, "After I am worn out and my lord (Abraham) is old, will I now have the pleasure of bearing a child?" I'm sure she thought, "Yeah, right! You're a day late and a dollar short, Lord!"

But, I love what the scripture reveals to us about Abraham's faith. Romans 4:19-21 declares, "He (Abraham) staggered not at the promise of God through unbelief; but was *strong in faith*, giving glory to God; and being *fully persuaded* that, what he (God) promised, he was fully able to perform." I emphasized the words that I want you to embrace in this passage.

This account of faith offers the remedy for unbelief:

- Do not question God's ability to perform the promise
- Your job is to personally activate your faith
- Remain fully persuaded against all odds

You see, Abraham and Sarah certainly had sound, physical reasons to refute the promise they received from God. They could have chosen to focus on their limited circumstances and disregarded the promise as nonsense, but Abraham chose to believe. His strong faith then moved his wife, Sarah, from a position of doubt to one of surrendered faith. At that very moment the promise of God was released from the spirit realm into the earthly realm. One year later, just as God had promised, Isaac was born unto these two faithful parents (Hebrews 11:11).

Your faith is the supernatural currency by which you make exchanges with heaven's storehouse. You exchange your faith for His promises! This is precisely why Jesus taught us in the Lord's Prayer found in Matthew 6:9-13, "May Your will in heaven be done on the earth." It is our responsibility to partner in the manifestation of God's perfect will through the process of faith.

In 2009, God commanded my husband to step away from the career he had in Nashville, Tennessee. Now, this was no small act of obedience. We certainly could have denied the voice of God speaking and chosen to focus on the many reasons why this did not sound like a very good idea. Steve had worked for this company for almost nine years, not to mention that America was in the depths of a recession. We were paying the mortgage on a five-thousand square foot house and had two teenagers, one presently in college. We had not anticipated this move. Nevertheless, God asked us to step out and prepare to enter into our promised land and we obeyed. This act of faith came with much ridicule from family, friends, and others in the community. People could not understand why anyone would do such a thing as this. And because they couldn't understand such faith, they mocked us and spread lies about us. Rumors reported that Steve had lost his job and that we were forced to sell our dream home and move to Texas.

I am only relaying this account to you that you may receive understanding: when you step out in faith, not everyone will understand. Do not allow their unbelief to persuade you, whatsoever! Remember, God is keeping the real score and He will cause you to shine with glory on the other side.

Others' Unbelief

Satan will use the unbelief of others to abort your faith. I am sure Abraham and Sarah had many in their sphere of influence who denied that God could give them a child in their old and barren state. Often, the words of disbelief and caution from those closest to you, such as a spouse, a family member, or close friend, can make it very difficult to remain in a position of constant faith. Others' unbelief can create noise and confusion in your head. Before you can continue along your journey of faith, there will be times that you will need to clear your atmosphere of anything that is not in alignment with your faith. Remain steadfastly focused on the promise you are believing for. You must create an "atmosphere of faith." We see Jesus doing this very thing when He went to the house of the centurion ruler Jairus, in Mark 5:35-42 (NIV):

"While Jesus was still speaking, some people came from the house of Jairus, the synagogue leader. 'Your daughter is dead,' they said. 'Why bother the teacher anymore?'

"Overhearing what they said, Jesus told him, 'Don't be afraid; just believe.'

"He did not let anyone follow him except Peter, James and John the brother of James. When they came to the home of the synagogue leader, Jesus saw a commotion, with people crying and wailing loudly. He went in and said to them, 'Why all this commotion and wailing? The child is not dead but asleep.' But they laughed at him.

"After he put them all out, he took the child's father and mother and the disciples who were with him, and went in where the child was. He took her by the hand and said to her, 'Talitha koum!' (which means 'Little girl, I say to you, get up!'). Immediately the girl stood up and began to walk around (she was twelve years old). At this they were completely astonished."

Before Jesus operated in faith, He created an atmosphere where faith could dwell by removing all the noise and negativity. He allowed only those who were in agreement with His faith to accompany Him into the room where the sick child lay. Jesus had twelve disciples, but notice that He took only three of them with Him. Your personal sphere may include many levels of friendships and widespread relations with different family members. While you

Faith is the supernatural currency by which you make exchanges with heaven's storehouse.

may love and respect them all, it is wise to only share your faith walk with people of like maturity and mindset. The adversary loves to hinder us through the mouths of those with small faith.

I am not sure what your "atmosphere of faith" looks like, but mine is constantly filled with faith promises from the Bible, encouraging sermons, books that feed my faith, records of personal prophecies, songs of praise and worship, and definitely my journal. I have kept a journal nearly every day since 1998. I love my quiet, intimate moments alone with Jesus where I record exactly what He is speaking into my heart. I have found journaling to be extremely beneficial to my faith walk because no matter how many details I think I will remember, I can never recall every one of them. So, it helps when I take the time to record God's promises and my personal heart dreams into my journals. There, I can always go back and read again and again the refreshing words, as well as the dates they were spoken. This keeps my faith alive and equips me with the strength I need to endure in a constant position of faith.

2. Wavering Faith

Another stumbling block to receiving the promises of God in your personal life is possessing faith that wavers. I'm sure you understand what I'm referring to. I think most of us fall into this broad category at some time or another.

Wavering faith acts much like a wave of the sea. One moment it is in and the next it is out, in and then out, in and out. Wavering faith trusts in the promise one day, but not the next. Wavering faith trusts God until the battle gets too difficult. Wavering faith trusts in the promise until tangible evidence begins to speak in support *against* the promise. It is then that we most often find ourselves second-guessing the promise. Faith wavers.

James 1:6-7 tells us: *"But let him ask in faith, nothing wavering. For he that wavereth is like a wave of the sea driven with the wind and tossed. For let not that man think that he shall receive any thing of the Lord."*

I generally believe that most Christians desire to walk in the blessed state of faith. I also believe that most believers set out to walk in faith at one time or another along their journey. Our carnal minds are the greatest enemy to faith. Those who waver are in a constant tug of war between spirit and flesh. It is easy to sit in a powerful church service, surrounded by like-minded believers, and build yourself up in faith. The wavering usually arises once you get back to your familiar territory. When you are no longer surrounded by the powerful sermon, the glorious songs, and the mighty shouts, reality has its way of creeping back into your mind, causing doubt. It's in the ordinary and familiar places that Satan whispers in our ears. He encourages us to take a good hard look at our circumstances, at our environment, at our marriage, at our past, at our limitations, and dare to believe that any good thing could ever come to us. But, remember, he is a liar! In fact, he is the creator and father of lies. Satan is already defeated, but he has not yet been sentenced. The world is his domain. But, he has only the authority over you that you give him.

I love the lesson learned from the passage of scripture found in Matthew 4:1-11 (NIV):

"Then Jesus was led by the Spirit into the wilderness to be tempted by the devil. After fasting forty days and forty nights, he was hungry. The tempter came to him and said, 'If you are the Son of God, tell these stones to become bread.'

"Jesus answered, 'It is written: Man shall not live on bread alone, but on every word that comes from the mouth of God.'

"Then the devil took him to the holy city and had him stand on the highest point of the temple. 'If you are the Son of God,' he said, 'throw yourself down. For it is written: He will command his angels concerning you, and they will lift you up in their hands, so that you will not strike your foot against a stone.'

"Jesus answered him, 'It is also written: Do not put the Lord your God to the test.'

"Again, the devil took him to a very high mountain and showed him all the kingdoms of the world and their splendor. 'All this I will give you,' he said, 'if you will bow down and worship me.'

"Jesus said to him, 'Away from me, Satan! For it is written: Worship the Lord your God, and serve him only.'

"Then the devil left him, and angels came and attended him."

Notice that Satan only came to Jesus after He had fasted and prayed for forty days and nights. This is because Satan is a coward. He already knows he has been defeated by the death and resurrection of Jesus Christ and that he has no real authority over the believer. So, his strategy is always the same: to approach the believer when he/she is isolated, hungry and weak. That's right. He came to Jesus when he was hungry, alone, and weak. As you walk in a lifestyle of faith it is so very important to:

- Surround yourself with believing friends
- Quench your appetite with the bread of life (the Bible)
- Have intimate communication with God

Secondly, Satan will always attempt to get you to second-guess your identity. Notice how Satan begins his act of devouring by saying to Jesus, "If you are the Son of God. . ." *IF?* By this, Satan is trying to cause Jesus to second-guess His identity because if he can get us to question our identity, then we will also question our purpose and authority. Yes, that's right. When you waver between your Christ-like identity and your earthly identity, you will waver in your faith every time.

Thirdly, Satan attacked Jesus by offering Him counterfeit blessings. He took Jesus to a very high mountain and showed Him all the kingdoms of this world and their splendor. He announced to Jesus that he would bless Him with all of this if He would bow down and worship him. This, my friend, is Satan's ultimate goal. He operates to manipulate people into forfeiting their eternal kingdom inheritance for his limited earthly pleasures. Many times, his strategy is successful because it is always easier to believe in what is tangible than to trust in the unseen.

I have to be real with you. There will be days that you do not "feel" hopeful about your faith. However, always remember that true faith is not based on feelings. It is cultivated in hope of that which is unseen. And Hope will not disappoint (Romans 5:5). When God gives you a promise, do not allow the waves of doubt to hinder your faith. Instead, grab your surfboard and ride atop each wave, always believing and always abounding in faith.

Do not waver between your identity in Christ and your earthly identity. Wavering erodes faith.

TESTIMONY

It was a quiet night in our apartment complex in Port Washington, Wisconsin. Our family had eaten a lovely dinner together and the supper dishes had all been washed. It was time to put our eighteen month old daughter to bed. Like most couples, Steve and I looked forward to our alone time at the end of the day. Alyse was always good about going to sleep on her own. She loved to play with her stuffed animals in the bed until falling asleep. I never expected that this night would be any different.

After several minutes of down time, I decided to check on our daughter. Only I did not find her sound asleep. I heard an odd noise. To this very day I can still recall it. Rushing over to Alyse, I found her lying on her back, choking. I screamed for Steve and immediately turned her over and began the process of relieving whatever was lodged in her throat.

"What is it?" I asked myself. I remembered Alyse playing with a few coins earlier that evening. I looked up and saw them lying on the dresser beside her bed. Had she swallowed one of the coins? In desperation, I tried to place my fingers down her throat and retrieve the hidden object, but to no avail. In panic, I lifted Alyse off the bed, into my arms and ran in my pajamas to the neighbor's apartment, screaming at the top of my lungs. The protective instincts of motherhood had certainly kicked in strongly. I practically beat the neighbor's door down. All the while shouting, "Call 911! My baby is dying! My baby is dying!"

Chris and Mary Ann were close friends. They were newlyweds with no children of their own and they were very fond of Alyse. In their calmness, they were able to call the ambulance. Upon arrival and working together with Alyse, she was diagnosed as having a seizure. A seizure? How? Why? I could not understand. Children do not just have seizures. After a rigorous night in the ER, we were released to go home. I did not want to go home. How could I sleep? I wanted Alyse to be under the supervision and care of trained professionals, but they assured me there was nothing more they could do. Alyse was scheduled to undergo a long list of tests the following week. The results showed that she had epilepsy. She was placed on a high dosage of Tegretol for every day of her life.

I remember thinking, "How will I ever be able to sleep again in my life?" The thought that she could have another seizure while I was asleep terrified me. For weeks, we took turns sleeping in her bed. Other times, we would make her a pallet on the floor beside ours. Alyse continued to have seizures. Often several a day. They always took place as she drifted off to sleep. It was difficult to be rocking her to sleep and watch her have a seizure right in our very arms. This continued day after day for the next eighteen months.

In the meanwhile, Steve and I relocated to Sauk Village, IL, a small town south of Chicago. We immediately became connected with a wonderful church. One weekend, I was invited to a Ladies Retreat. It was hard to leave Alyse, but I really felt God nudging me to go. On the second night of the retreat, during the service, our pastor's wife prophesied to me saying, "God wants you to trust Him. He has healed your little girl." Even in my childlike spiritual condition this was all I needed to hear. If God said it, then I believed it.

I came straight home, explained it to Steve, and we took our three year old daughter off her daily regimen of epilepsy medication. We also scheduled a routine EEG, a test to measure the electrical activity of her brain. During the consultation, I told the physician that we had taken Alyse off of the Tegretol medication she had been taking for eighteen months because she was healed. Within the hour, my declaration of faith was proven to be true according to the test results. For the first time since Alyse had been diagnosed with epilepsy, she showed no signs of any

abnormal brain activity on the EEG. However, the physician was very alarmed that we had chosen to take Alyse off the medication against the approval of a board certified physician, stating that we could have done more harm to her than good. We learned it is not wise to remove someone from medication cold-turkey like that, but we did not care because we experienced a miracle right before our very eyes.

Alyse never took medication for epilepsy again. Several months went by without a seizure. Our testimony rang out everywhere we went. God received all the glory for healing our daughter and I felt like I could run through a troop and jump over a wall! However, my faith would soon be tested again.

One fall night in October, our daughter requested to sleep on a pallet beside our bed. This was a treat for her, so we happily agreed. Deep into the night, I was awakened by an all-too familiar sound. Terrified and not wanting to really know, I reached over to turn on the lamp. There, I found Alyse having another seizure. I held her in my arms and prayed over her until it ceased. I cannot explain just how I felt. My faith was crushed and all hope was adrift.

The next morning, discouraged and feeling like a fool, I called my pastor's wife who had prophesied to me. I could not understand why God would let me tell everyone Alyse was healed if she was not. I was embarrassed. My precious sister, who has since gone on to be with the Lord, gave me life-changing news that took my faith to a whole new level. She said, "This is only a test brought on by Satan. Your daughter is healed! Keep believing, Jeneen."

Then, I realized the depth of 2 Corinthians 5:7 which says, "We walk by faith and not by sight." I had to learn that often what we see in the natural is not what is taking place in the spiritual. It no longer mattered that I saw my daughter having a seizure with my physical eyes. All that mattered to me now was that God had said she was healed.

> This revelation added a new level of deep, deep trust in my Father. Romans 3:4 says, "Let God be true, and every man a liar."
>
> For years I did not really comprehend this scripture, but I want you to fully understand what it is saying. Anything, whether it is a man, a thought, or a sickness–anything that exalts itself against the word that God has spoken to you is a liar.
>
> I am happy to report that our daughter is now twenty-six years old and she has never had another seizure in her entire life. She is beautiful and uses her gifts and hands to serve and heal others around the nation as a traveling registered nurse! To our great God be the glory!

If you find yourself in a position of wavering faith right now, there is no need to beat yourself up about it. All hope is not lost. Mark 9:24 says: "I DO believe, but help me overcome my unbelief!" (NLT) Wavering faith is common, but not profitable. Take a few moments to analyze what causes you to waver back and forth in your faith. Are you trusting too strongly in your tangible circumstances? Is Satan whispering in your ear? Is he tempting you to question your identity? Is he persuading you to accept his temporal offer, rather than remain in steady faith to receive the perfect will God has for your life? Educating yourself on the devil's schemes will bring awareness for newfound faith strategies and defeat the wavering.

3. Lack of Perseverance

You may not operate in the spirit of unbelief. Perhaps you have even conquered the tendency to waver. But, now, you find yourself in quite a predicament. Long, long ago, God gave you a powerful promise and you stood firm in your faith, but that was twenty-five years ago! You used to really trust God for the promise, but as each passing year ended without fulfillment you simply gave up.

It is true–"Hope deferred makes the heart sick" (Proverbs 13:12). However, the rest of the verse declares, "But when the promise comes it is a tree of life." I love how another translation reads:

"Unrelenting disappointment makes the heart sick, but when dreams come true, there is life and joy."

We must remember: Faith is the substance of things hoped for! And when our hope gets delayed we can go through all sorts of emotions. Emotions can be inaccurate.

Know this: All Faith Will Be Tested!

But, there is a reason for this. James 1:3-4 (NIV): *"Because you know that the testing of your faith produces perseverance. Let perseverance finish its work so that you may be mature and complete, not lacking anything."*

Allow perseverance to complete the process of spiritual maturity in you. Do not give up and, for heaven's sake, do not try to intervene. In the early stages of your walk of faith, when resistance or trying times come knocking on your door, you may feel the urgency to step in and become part of the solution you are seeking. Sometimes, you may even look to another person to provide the long-awaited answer. It is at these times that you need to become cautiously aware of the arm of flesh. Endure and continue to trust God for your promise all the more. Keep self and human comprehension out of the faith scenario at all cost. When your familiar circumstances begin to speak against the promise of God, do what I do. I simply ask myself, "What did GOD say, Jeneen?" I have trained my mind to acknowledge whatever GOD tells me as my new reality, NOT what I see in my natural surroundings.

We receive great example of this from Elijah in the 18th chapter of 1 Kings. To shed a bit of background on the story: There was a great famine in the land due to the lack of rainfall for a period of three years. It was, in fact, Elijah himself who had prophesied the great and terrible drought to King Ahab. In the third year of the famine/drought, God calls Elijah to present himself before King Ahab once more. There, he performs a showdown between the prophets of Baal and the one True God. Of course, we know how that turned out. God showed Himself strong through fire and consumed not only the sacrifice upon Elijah's altar, but also the water

What God says must be your only reality.

surrounding the sacrifice. Once God is declared the one true and living God, He tells Elijah to declare to King Ahab that he hears the sound of the abundance of rain.

Now, remember, it has not rained one drop in three years. Without reluctance, Elijah declares that he hears the abundance of rain, but in the natural there was no rain. God spoke a prophetic promise unto Elijah and Elijah received the word from God without ANY evidence to support his statement.

Elijah knelt to earnestly pray, just as many of you have. Then, he sent his servant to see if there was any evidence of rain? But, there was no evidence. There was no natural sign in the sky. Once again, Elijah kneeled to pray and once again he sent his servant to scope out the sky. Still, there was no evidence of rain. There was not even a cloud. Six different times, the prophet Elijah sent his servant to look for some natural sign of evidence that what God had spoken to him would come to pass. And six different times, the servant returned with disappointing news.

What would you have done? Better yet, what are you doing NOW with no natural evidence to encourage you and serve as a sign that you are not crazy and that you really did hear God speak to your spirit? After six attempts at answered prayer, do you give up or continue to trust in the promise of God?

On Elijah's seventh attempt, his servant returned with some good news. He said, "I see a rain cloud the size of a man's hand." Before long, the heavens were turned dark with clouds and wind and a great rain arose! What would have happened if Elijah would have gotten discouraged by the sixth time and said, "Forget it! I must have just *thought* I heard the Word of the Lord?" He would have never realized that His answer was in the seventh attempt. He was on the verge of his miracle. Had he not persevered and trusted that what God said was the only reality, then he would not have received the promise.

Six attempts at trusting God for the manifestation of your promise can be draining. During our time of waiting, it may appear that God is late, but, *"The Lord is not slack concerning his promise, as some men count slackness"* (2 Peter 3:9).

In our concept of time, it can seem like God is sometimes late. In the 11th chapter of the book of John, we find the story of Lazarus who was sick and almost at the point of death. Jesus loved Lazarus. He was His dear friend and when Mary and Martha called for the attention of Jesus, they sent for Him quickly so that He might lay hands on their brother, healing him and saving him from death. But, when Jesus was notified of the condition of His friend, John tells us that Jesus remained two more full days in the location He was at instead of rushing to Lazarus' side.

In my early years in the church, I was always taught that God is never late, but it would appear in this depiction of Lazarus' death that God was, in fact, late because once Jesus got there, Lazarus was already dead in the grave. He had been dead three days and the Word alludes to the fact that he was already beginning to stink! In our context and comprehension of time, Jesus was late! End of discussion! But, verses 4 and 5 lend truth to our drama.

"This sickness will not end in death. No, it is for God's glory so that God's Son may be glorified through it. Now Jesus loved Martha and her sister and Lazarus. So when he heard that Lazarus was sick, he stayed where he was two more days."

Does that seem like love to you? No! Neither does it seem like love when we cry out to God for answers to our prayers, but neither hear nor witness any answers in return. However, God is not operating in our realm of time. Our prayers are answered when we least expect them to be, that Jesus may be glorified in the earth before a great many witnesses. That is why we must persevere, my dear friend. We cannot give up and throw in the towel. We can always trust that God will fulfill His promise to us in His own time. Even when your situation looks dead. Even when the door of your situation already looks like it has been closed! Jesus is the master at bringing glory to His Father. He loves to answer our prayers and deliver the perfect remedy to our situations against all odds. Never, ever give up. Never throw in the towel. Continue to stand in faith for what God has promised you–against all odds!

Hebrews 10:35-36 is one of my all-time favorite scriptures: "Do not throw away your confidence, which has great reward. (Here's the key) For you have need of endurance (perseverance), so that after you have done the will of God you will receive the promise."

TESTIMONY

I come from a fantastic line of women in my family who really know how to cook and bake. My mother taught me to prepare great meals at a very young age; fried pork chops, homemade mashed potatoes, fried corn, macaroni and cheese with real Velveeta, and fresh biscuits. I better stop there, my mouth is watering already...

I sort of pride myself as successor of these great cooks and bakers in my family. A few years ago, I had a night of setback. I call this my chicken story.

I decided I wanted to bake two whole chickens for supper. The rotisserie at Walmart always made them appear so delicious and appealing as I passed by and, although I had cooked chicken every other possible way in the past, I realized I had never baked a whole chicken myself. I retrieved a great recipe from the internet and purchased every necessary ingredient. Diligent to follow every step, I basted the chickens with natural herbs, set the oven to 350 degrees, and loaded it with what I was sure would become a family favorite.

My starving family waited in anticipation as the two hour cooking time slowly ticked away. Everyone's favorite side dish was carefully prepared to compliment this great entrée. After calling everyone to the table and humbly blessing this grub (which was sure to fill our stomachs with utter fulfillment), I pulled the perfectly golden chickens from the oven. At last, we sat together at the table to partake and, to my disappointment, the chickens were raw! I could not believe my eyes, nor could I understand! My mind retraced every step I had taken. I KNOW I followed that recipe to the T and was careful to do everything just right. How could these chickens appear so ready and yet be so completely not ready? Needless to say, we could not eat the chickens! Nor, have I attempted to bake another one since. It was in the early morning hours that my heavenly Father awakened me and spoke. "Jeneen, I want to teach you something through the chickens."

I said, "Sure, Father, what?"

He replied, "You know how you did everything you were supposed to do to those chickens to yield a fabulous return?"

I said, "Yes, Lord."

He continued, "And, to the natural eye, they appeared ready, correct?"

"Yes, Lord. They sure did."

"That is how life is at times, my daughter. You may think it is time for something to manifest that you have been praying about. You may have done everything you know to do to bring this new thing to pass. The circumstances may even appear as perfect timing, but it's just not ready, yet."

Being willing to roll with God's timing is crucial. So often in life, we pray about things and cannot understand why they have not come to pass. Circumstances may appear ready and your patience may be dwindling, but God knows the perfect time to bring things to pass in your life. Sometimes, you may think you are ready, when He knows you are not. If God did everything we asked Him to do in our own timing, most of us would fall flat on our faces in failure because we were not properly trained nor prepared for the task ahead.

Learn to trust God's timing. When He seems late, He isn't. And when your timing seems right, it isn't! God alone is omniscient–the all-knowing, wise One! He is aware of things you cannot know and He is following His own carefully-constructed plan for your life.

May Psalm 37:5 encourage you today: *"Commit your way to the Lord, Trust in Him And He shall bring it to pass!"*

Promises are assigned to seasons in our lives. You may receive the promise from God in one season and experience breakthrough

and manifestation of the promise in yet another. Never surrender! This journey takes more than your own firm resolve and determination. Success and victory will require the enabling grace and power of the Holy Spirit. You cannot successfully do life alone. Holy Spirit is your truth, your teacher, your strength, your perseverance, and your every victor.

Rhythm Reflections

1. Jesus said, "You have believed because you have seen. But, Blessed are those who believe who have not seen." What do you trust God for right now without any earthly evidence to support your faith?

2. What promises have you dismissed as nonsense because there simply is no tangible evidence to encourage you to believe?

3. Sarah initially laughed at the promise of God because it seemed impossible. Abraham's faith encouraged her to surrender her doubt. What does your atmosphere of faith currently look like? Do you surround yourself with people of great faith?

4. We create a dwelling place for faith as we remove all the noise and negativity. Do you need to remove any person or thing from your atmosphere?

5. Wavering is common, but is not profitable. From where does most of your wavering originate?

6. Spiritual hunger, isolation, and weakness contribute to wavering one's faith. Of these, which do you need to pay more time and attention to overcome?

7. What counterfeit offers have you accepted from Satan instead of waiting on God's perfect will for your life?

8. *"I believe, Lord, but help my unbelief."* In what ways does this verse reflect your personal situation?

9. *"Hope deferred makes the heart sick."* What hopes have you waited for that leave you feeling miserably sick? Are there promises from this chapter that you can cling to that will strengthen your faith in this area?

10. *"Do not throw away your confidence, which has great reward. For you have need of endurance, so that after you have done the will of God you will receive the promise."* The key to this verse is the need for endurance. What is God asking you to believe for?

Prayer

Father God, Your Son came to earth as my ransom. He suffered and victoriously rose again to provide me an abundant life! I realize now that it is my responsibility to partner with You in bringing Your perfect will to pass in my life. I desire to trust You more and more. I believe, but Holy Spirit, help also my unbelief. Thank You for teaching me these important keys to powerful, consistent faith. Seal this knowledge upon my heart, that I may forever be conscious of the enemy's strategies. The best is yet to come for me, Lord. YOU make me excited! I love You. In Jesus' Name I pray. Amen.

Use the space below to write any specific prayer requests you have:

Chapter 8
Dream!

"They said to one another, 'Here comes this dreamer!'"
–Genesis 37:19

WHAT CAN I say? I am one of those–a dreamer! I always have been, even as a little girl. No matter what situation I find myself in, there is always a greater dream within my heart. Dreaming, for me, has never been the product of discontentment! I simply thrive on the confidence of knowing I am a Child of the Most High, therefore: "all things are mine and nothing is impossible."

Dreaming: To believe for something beyond what you can presently see. Sounds a lot like FAITH, huh? In 2006, this dreaming of mine went to a whole new level as I began to witness my dreams coming to pass. With burning passion, I found myself even designating certain days just for dreaming! Often, I would get into my car and set out to dream of greater territory, greater prosperity, and greater influence! It was not long before my dreaming rubbed off on personal friends and family members. Together, we would often stop what we were doing and say, "Let's go dreaming today!"

Now, I know what some are probably thinking right now. "Who has time to dream? I'm way too busy for that! Why waste time wishing for things you cannot have? I can sure think of better ways to spend my time!"

Yes, I do receive quite a bit of persecution for dreaming, but it never bothers me. I simply dream a bigger dream! At first, I didn't understand why Holy Spirit always seemed to guide me in this direction. In comparison to others, I certainly appeared to be an odd cookie. However, one day, God graciously chose to give me understanding on the matter through a book I was reading by Stephen K. DeSilva: *Money and the Prosperous Soul* (Chosen Books, 2010).

> "Our dreams matter. I believe God engineered each of us to dream–to envision the fulfillment of our hopes and desires. In fact, dreaming is so vital for us that without it, none of us will reach our full potential in life. A dream is like a buoy that lifts us above mediocrity and monotony. Yet even more fundamentally, dreaming keeps us ALIVE, because it connects us to vision. The New American Standard Bible translates Proverbs 29:18 this way, Where there is no vision, the people 'let go,' 'neglect,' or 'give up.' The final result is that we perish and it all happens through lack of vision."

Regardless of what you may have been taught, our God is interested in more about your life than simply how you serve Him and how many people you lead to salvation. He cares about the dreams and the desires of your heart. We all have dreams and desires, but oftentimes they are regressed to the back of our minds and forgotten about like lost treasures.

As an excited Father, God is thrilled to fulfill your dreams and desires when they line up with His will and timing. A few years after I had been walking with the Lord, I was reading Psalm 37:4: "Delight yourself in the Lord, and he will give you the desires of your heart." Suddenly, a light came on and I not only realized that God was the fulfillment of my dreams and desires, but that He was actually the One *who had given me these dreams and desires in the first place!* I learned that when I find delight in my relationship with Him, He then fills my life with the desires and dreams He wishes to grant me. This revolutionized my thinking about the many things I dreamed of having, the number of places I dreamed of going, and the goals I had set to accomplish in the kingdom. Suddenly, I realized these were more than things "I" desired. They were actually the desires and dreams my heavenly Father desired for me. So, He lovingly placed them in my heart and caused me to also desire them.

This kind of thinking fueled my hope because I understood

that if God gave me these desires and dreams, then I can be confident that He will also fulfill them. None of my dreams or desires will go unfulfilled. I have waited as long as 20 years for certain things to come to pass, but if He places it inside my heart, I know it will eventually happen. Therefore, when we speak of dreams and desires being fulfilled, it is important to respect the timing of God. He does not work in our time frame. Sometimes, He will tell me that He is going to do a thing quickly for me, only for me to realize His "quickly" meant 7 years later. When you are dealing with a God who has infinite time, the words quickly, suddenly, and soon begin to take on new meaning. Aligning your life with God's proper timing is part of the spiritual maturity process.

TESTIMONY

Remember the dream house we built that I wrote about previously? Well, while we were building that house, before it was even completed, God spoke to me as I sat on my mother's screened-in porch one sunny afternoon. He said, "You will live in this house for a season and be very blessed. Then, I will require it of you." Three and a half years later, I finally understood what He meant by "require it of me." In January of 2010, God asked us to sell our dream home, complete with nearly all of its contents, and move to Dallas, Texas. Steve and I planned to rent a home in Texas for a while. We thought it was the wise thing to do because we had never lived in Texas so we were not sure we would even like living there. We were not sure if Steve would enjoy working at this new company and with it being a recession we thought it wise to learn the market in our area before purchasing a house.

For many weeks, Steve looked for the perfect rental home for our family. Twice, he flew me to Texas in hopes of accelerating the hunt, but nothing we looked at ever felt just right. One afternoon, God said, "Make a list of everything you desire or dream of for this rental home." If you know

God is thrilled to fulfill your dreams and desires when they align with His will and timing.

me very well, then you realize that I am a woman who always knows exactly what she wants. So, without hesitation, I compiled my list. I would like:

- at least 2,500 square feet
- hardwood floors
- granite countertops
- a bonus room
- a pool with a fountain flowing into it

None of the houses available had the features I desired. However, one Sunday, I received a call from the pastor of the church Steve and I had visited the two weekends I flew to Texas. The voice on the other end of the line said, "I think I may have a house you might be interested in." Within hours, we were touring the home and I was grinning from ear to ear. The house had absolutely everything I had desired on my list. We signed the leasing contract and I headed back to Nashville to scoop up the remaining few belongings we possessed. I testified to everyone I knew of God's goodness and how He was such a detailed God to give me every desire I had for a rental home. On the final drive back to Texas from Nashville, I heard the accusing voice of my adversary proclaim, "This house doesn't have EVERYTHING you wrote on your list!" In my excitement over the house, it had never occurred to me that the pool did not have a fountain that flowed over into it. I realize that this may sound stupid to you, but I was instantly filled with condemnation. I am such a woman of my word and it killed me that I had given a false to testimony to so many. My heart was burdened.

As soon as I arrived in Texas, I drove straight to the rental house to drop off our big yellow Labrador in the fenced-in back yard. I walked around the side of the house to gaze upon the beautiful pool and to my own amazement, there was a peaceful flowing fountain spilling over into the pool. My eyes filled with tears. The owner of the house stepped outside to greet me. He said, "The fountain wasn't working when you toured the house the other day, but I had it repaired for you!"

TESTIMONY

As you know, Steve and I were married very quickly at seventeen years of age. We owned nothing except the clothes in our closets. Getting an engagement ring was totally out of the question. We purchased a thin gold band for each other and happily proceeded with the wedding. Steve carried the receipt of this memorable purchase in his wallet for many years after we were married until it became unrecognizable!

It doesn't matter who you are, I believe every woman desires an engagement ring from her Prince Charming. Even though I knew Steve could not afford to buy me one, it did not remove the desire I had in my heart for a ring to mark this glorious occasion. After we had been married a year or so, I received a diamond engagement ring for Christmas. It was a quarter carat marquise. I was thrilled.

As the years passed, my desire for a bigger, prettier ring grew. Steve and I would often browse through the jewelry stores dreaming. Year after year after year, I made my desire a matter of prayer before the Lord. Oh, I could have had a very nice ring, but I dreamed of a huge ring and was quite content with the ring I owned until the appointed time for my desire would come to pass. Many years passed by and we were quickly approaching our twenty-fifth wedding anniversary. I really wanted to have my dream ring before our anniversary, but we were not in financial shape to purchase the expensive ring I dreamt of. We had just put our daughter through nursing school and had our son in the middle of his college education. Still, God knew the dream of my heart. He knows everything about me. And, He knows everything about YOU too.

On the fourth of July, 2013–two months before our

> 25th wedding anniversary–my mom visited an aunt of mine at her home on Hilton Head Island. While there, she overheard my aunt on the phone discussing how she had a three carat diamond ring she desired to sell. She had purchased the ring as an investment in 1976 from a musician who needed some quick cash. After making the purchase, she placed the ring in her safety deposit box at the bank and that's exactly where it remained for the next thirty-seven years! She had never even worn it! To make this long story short, Mom told my aunt that I might be interested in purchasing the ring. She insured and overnighted the ring to me. When Steve opened the box, he was amazed. The carat, cut, and clarity of the ring was everything I had asked for. He purchased the ring from my aunt with cash. He then, permitted me to make it uniquely my own by allowing me to choose the setting I desired to hold this beautiful diamond.
>
> On September 10, 2013, on a beach in Cabo San Lucas, Steve placed this new ring of my dreams on my finger, in a private ceremony where we renewed our love and vows to one another for our 25th wedding anniversary. It was truly a dream come true!
>
> Friends, this diamond had been put away in that safety deposit box just for me when I was only five years old. My aunt had no idea what she was actually buying the ring for at the time, but God did! He is the fulfillment of our dreams. Abba Father loves us so much.

I could go on and on with testimonies of God giving and fulfilling the dreams and desires of my heart, but I want to discuss a much different type of dream with you. As I stated above, one definition of the word dream is "to believe for something beyond what presently exists in your life." The second definition of dream is "a series of mental images and emotions occurring during sleep."

I believe every human being possesses the ability to dream while they sleep. In fact, this morning as I lay restless upon my bed, I was reminded that even my dog dreams. With eyes fully closed and while sound asleep, Caesar began quietly barking under his breath and his paws started to move back and forth as if he was running after something. (Knowing him like I do, I would say he was dreaming of chasing "someone" instead of something. He's quite the protective type.)

Have you ever watched a newborn baby who was sound asleep begin to grin? His or her eyes begin to move with rapid motion, while jerking an arm or a leg. I often wonder what babies dream about? I mean how many images and emotions have they experienced in the short number of days they have existed in this life?

My point is that we all dream, but the kind of dreams we have may differ one from another. Sometimes, I experience crazy dreams that do not make any sense at all. I believe this kind of dream is nothing more than my subconscious reliving images, scenes, actions, and emotions I may have already experienced in life. Other times, I have had really scary dreams that disturbed me greatly. You know the ones? We refer to them as nightmares. This kind of dream was more prevalent when I was a young girl. I used to love watching horror movies. My brothers and I saw every horror movie released in the 80s. When it was time to sleep, I sure paid a price for subjecting my mind to these evil images. Fear often paralyzed me. The visions I saw and the nightmares I was awakened by were horrific.

"The eye is the lamp of the body. If your eyes are healthy, your whole body will be full of light. But if your eyes are unhealthy, your whole body will be full of darkness. If then the light within you is darkness, how great is that darkness!" (Matthew 6:22-23 NIV)

"Above all else, guard your heart, for everything you do flows from it" (Proverbs 4:23 NIV).

The course of your life will follow the direction of your heart. That is why it matters greatly what you subject your heart to through the windows of your eyes and ears. Since surrendering my life to the Lord and choosing to meditate on things that are true, honorable, just, pure, lovely, and excellent, I no longer experience these nightmares or the paralyzing fear.

Still, there is yet another kind of dream that many are not aware of. I call them God-dreams. Yes, one way that God chooses to speak to us and heighten our faith is through dream.

"For God speaketh once, yea twice, yet man perceiveth it not. In a dream, in a vision of the night, when deep sleep falleth upon men, in slumberings upon the bed; Then he openeth the ears of men, and sealeth their instruction, That he may withdraw man from his purpose, and hide pride from man. He keepeth back his soul from the pit, and his life from perishing by the sword" (Job 33:14-18).

God-dreams are given to us for the purpose of directing, warning, and/or preparing. Perhaps you have also experienced God-dreams, but you did not perceive them as such. Instead, you may have dismissed His message, chalking it up as "just another dream." I'm sure I did this quite a bit in my younger days until I began to distinguish between a regular dream and a God-dream. I began to notice that when I have a regular dream, I can only remember bits and pieces of the events in my mind once I awaken, but whenever I experience a God-dream I can recall every single detail for years to come. I do not always understand what each detail means right away, but I still remember each one.

These dreams have become so valuable to me that now when I lay down to sleep at night or even nap throughout my day, I ask God to speak to me through my dreams. This is not absurdity, but truth. After all, a dream of this kind is exactly how God prepared Joseph for the birth of Jesus in Matthew 1:18-21 (NIV, emphasis mine).

"This is how the birth of Jesus the Messiah came about. His mother Mary was pledged to be married to Joseph, but before they came together, she was found to be pregnant through the Holy Spirit. Because Joseph her husband was faithful to the law, and yet did not want to expose her to public disgrace, he had in mind to divorce her quietly.

*"But after he had considered this, **an angel of the Lord appeared to him in a dream** and said, 'Joseph son of David, do not be afraid to take Mary home as your wife, because what is conceived*

in her is from the Holy Spirit. She will give birth to a son, and you are to give him the name Jesus, because he will save his people from their sins.'"

This God-dream not only told of the forthcoming of Christ, but also provided Joseph insight into "his purpose" in the process. The dream impacted Joseph so much that he never questioned the direction he received from the dream.

In the 2nd chapter of Matthew, Joseph was given another God-dream. This time the dream provided him with a specific warning. Matthew 2:1-15 (emphasis mine):

"After Jesus was born in Bethlehem in Judea, during the time of King Herod, Magi from the east came to Jerusalem and asked, 'Where is the one who has been born king of the Jews? We saw his star when it rose and have come to worship him.'

"When King Herod heard this he was disturbed, and all Jerusalem with him. When he had called together all the people's chief priests and teachers of the law, he asked them where the Messiah was to be born. 'In Bethlehem in Judea,' they replied, 'for this is what the prophet has written:

"But you, Bethlehem, in the land of Judah, are by no means least among the rulers of Judah; for out of you will come a ruler who will shepherd my people Israel.'

"Then Herod called the Magi secretly and found out from them the exact time the star had appeared. He sent them to Bethlehem and said, 'Go and search carefully for the child. As soon as you find him, report to me, so that I too may go and worship him.'

"After they had heard the king, they went on their way, and the star they had seen when it rose went ahead of them until it stopped over the place where the child was. When they saw the star, they were overjoyed. On coming to the house, they saw the child with his mother Mary, and they bowed down and worshiped him. Then they opened their treasures and presented him with gifts of gold, frankincense and myrrh. And ***having been warned in a dream*** *not to go back to Herod, they returned to their country by another route.*

"Now when they had departed, behold, an angel of the Lord

***appeared to Joseph in a dream** and said, 'Rise, take the child and his mother, and flee to Egypt, and remain there until I tell you, for Herod is about to search for the child, to destroy him.' And he rose and took the child and his mother by night and departed to Egypt and remained there until the death of Herod. This was to fulfill what the Lord had spoken by the prophet, 'Out of Egypt I called my son.'"*

God-dreams allow us to see events in this life from God's perspective. Our only daughter, who is a Registered Nurse, decided she was very interested in becoming a traveling nurse. She enrolled with a traveling nurse agency and chose her first assignment in the beautiful state of Oregon. I have moved 24 times in my 44 years of living, so my daughter's decision to move did not alarm me. However, the idea of her living 39 hours from us led me to seek God for His will and approval on the matter. One night while I slept, God spoke to me in a dream saying, "Interstate 5 is My will for Alyse." I heard His message very loud and clear, but what did it mean? I had no idea where Interstate 5 was? For that matter, I had no idea if there even was an Interstate 5. In the wee hours of the night, I googled Interstate 5 and found that this interstate ran parallel to the entire west coast of the United States, running right through the exact city Alyse had chosen to move to. God affirmed my daughter's decision and cared enough for me to fill my mind with His total peace.

TESTIMONY

In November 2012, God gave me a dream. In this dream, Steve and I were suddenly buying a new house on a lot of acreage. One important detail that stood out to me was the year the house was built–1910. In the dream, Steve and I were buying this old house so suddenly that we had no idea it had an in-ground pool in the backyard. Several friends showed up at the house to help us move in. Alyse and Bryce were also present. In the next scene we were all sitting in the living room of the house when the walls began

God-dreams allow us to see events in this life from God's perspective.

to shake. I looked at the others sitting around me and very calmly proclaimed, "We are having an earthquake." It was very strange because the walls of the house were vibrating, but none of the pictures were falling off the walls. None of the furniture was moving. Everyone remained seated and calm. Suddenly, the house we were seated in swung off of its foundation, just as a door swings on hinges, and sat upon a new foundation. The dream ended.

When I woke up, I was troubled for a bit. This dream had occurred during a time of isolation God had me in and at first glance I wasn't sure if God was trying to warn me that we had really gotten away from the spiritual foundation we had so wisely built our house upon or what?

It took a while to understand the true meaning and purpose of the dream. Now, three years later, the message is very clear. God was warning me that He was getting ready to shake things up in our lives and shift us into a brand new place. The calmness of the earthquake was a reminder from God that, although He planned to shake things up and rearrange our beliefs for a more firm foundation, it would not be accomplished through chaos and tragedy. No, this shift would take place in peace. He led me to study the numbers 19 and 10...the year the house was built...and when I did I learned that 19 means faith and 10 means testimony. Navigation through this shaking and shifting would come by faith and would end in a great testimony for our family.

I once had someone in my life who I considered to be a very good friend. She brought a lot of baggage into our friendship due to a lack of true identity as a daughter of Daddy God. In my nurturing nature, I always overlooked the load and tried to be extra gracious when things were heavy. She was the jealous, competitive type with deep-rooted insecurities. This caused much pain in my life and eventually ended up affecting my ministry.

God began to deal with me about the necessity of setting proper boundaries. For eighteen months, He encouraged me to walk away from this relationship and cut all ties. For the longest time, I was afraid to respond to His direction because I have always imagined my God as a God of restoration. I could not see how ending this friendship could possibly be His will for my life. I sought His face continually on the matter. God sent confirmation to me by the mouth of three witnesses and also gave me a stern warning–"If you do not cut ties with this person, you will never have what I have for you in the future." With this stern rebuke, I took God at His word and cut all ties. My heart hurt to do so, but as I cried out to God, He spoke to me once again saying, "This person may be a friend to a lot of people, but unfortunately she is not a good friend to you. Walk away."

I worried about how this "cutting ties" process would go. "I am not a mean-spirited person. How do I do this, God?"

He replied, "She will call you three times and after that she will never call you again." That is exactly what happened. The process ended up being smooth and easy. In fact, this person never even once texted, called, or emailed to ask why I might be doing what I was doing. To me, that spoke volumes!

After much time had passed, my heart began to miss my friend and I felt a longing to reconcile. I muttered within myself saying, "Perhaps she has changed, Lord? Maybe we can be better friends now?"

That night, God gave me a dream and revealed to me that my friend had not changed one bit, nor had she learned anything from our friendship break-up. God clearly directed me NOT to reconcile.

God has given me many dreams about my future destiny in ministry. These dreams are full of the grand things yet to be seen. In times past, I made the vital mistake of sharing these dreams with others surrounding me. I learned valuable lessons:

- Not everyone will be as excited about your dreams as you are.
- Dreamers attract jealousy.
- Dreamers are mocked.
- Dreamers attract leeches who desire to ride your coat tail.
- Some people are assigned to your life, but others will attach themselves to your life. Learn to recognize the difference.

- Some people will try to abort your dreams through their own unbelief.

Consider this a warning. Be very cautious who you decide to share your dreams with. This lesson can best be illustrated in the life of Joseph from Genesis 37:2-19 (NIV, emphasis mine):

"This is the account of Jacob's family line.

"Joseph, a young man of seventeen, was tending the flocks with his brothers, the sons of Bilhah and the sons of Zilpah, his father's wives, and he brought their father a bad report about them.

"Now Israel loved Joseph more than any of his other sons, because he had been born to him in his old age; and he made an ornate robe for him. When his brothers saw that their father loved him more than any of them, they hated him and could not speak a kind word to him.

"Joseph had a dream, and when he told it to his brothers, they hated him all the more.

"He said to them, 'Listen to this dream I had: We were binding sheaves of grain out in the field when suddenly my sheaf rose and stood upright, while your sheaves gathered around mine and bowed down to it.'

"His brothers said to him, 'Do you intend to reign over us? Will you actually rule us?' ***And they hated him all the more*** *because of his dream and what he had said.*

"Then he had another dream, and he told it to his brothers. *'Listen,' he said, 'I had another dream, and this time the sun and moon and eleven stars were bowing down to me.'*

"When he told his father as well as his brothers, his father rebuked him and said, 'What is this dream you had? Will your mother and I and your brothers actually come and bow down to the ground before you?' ***His brothers were jealous of him****, but his father kept the matter in mind.*

"Now his brothers had gone to graze their father's flocks near Shechem, and Israel said to Joseph, 'As you know, your brothers are grazing the flocks near Shechem. Come, I am going to send you to them.'

"'Very well,' he replied.

"So he said to him, 'Go and see if all is well with your brothers and with the flocks, and bring word back to me.' Then he sent him off from the Valley of Hebron.

"When Joseph arrived at Shechem, a man found him wandering around in the fields and asked him, 'What are you looking for?'

"He replied, 'I'm looking for my brothers. Can you tell me where they are grazing their flocks?'

"'They have moved on from here,' the man answered. 'I heard them say, Let's go to Dothan.'

"So Joseph went after his brothers and found them near Dothan. But they saw him in the distance, and before he reached them, they plotted to kill him.

***"'Here comes that dreamer!' they said to each other. 'Come now, let's kill him and throw him into one of these cisterns and say that a ferocious animal devoured him.** Then we'll see what comes of his dreams.'"*

Joseph shared his dreams with his brothers, an act not so out of the ordinary. The union between family members should support the dreams and victories of all involved. Note here that the brothers weren't offended that Joseph had a dream. They were offended at the content of his dream because it concluded that Joseph would reign higher than they would.

In his excitement, the dreams Joseph shared caused resentment, envy, and jealousy in those closest to him. This same insecurity, rivalry, and competitiveness is still very much a part of the Body of Christ. We must understand that while those accounted for in the Body of Christ are saved, not all have allowed Christ to mature and sanctify their carnal mindsets and, while not always intentional, these are the ones who can hurt you the most.

I love how David puts it in the psalms.

"For it is not an enemy who insults me–I could have handled that. Nor is it someone who hates me and who now arises against me –I could have hidden myself from him, but it is YOU–a man whom I treated as my equal, my personal confidant, my close friend" (Psalm

55:12-13).

In humility, remain mindful of others before you step out and share your God-dreams! Ponder these hidden treasures deep within your heart, but do not share them with others unless the Lord leads you to do so.

Also, be sure your time and energy is spent on dreaming your own dream. Never try to latch on and live the dream of someone else. You will never be able to do it. This will only cause failure and frustration in your life. God has anointed you with the proper amount of grace to enable you to fulfill all that He has created you to do, but He has not anointed you to fulfill the calling of anyone else.

May you enter into His rest now–a place where you no longer feel the need to compare your life to the life and calling of anyone else. You are unique and when you seek after Daddy God with your whole heart, He will be faithful to guide you to green pastures. Look out, world! I see new dreamers arising. May you be blessed in all of His great plans for your life.

Rhythm Reflections

1. Do you consider yourself to be a dreamer? If so, how do you reflect on the dreams you have?

2. "Delight yourself in the Lord; And He will give you the desires of your heart" (Psalm 37:4 NASB). What is your interpretation of this scripture?

3. Does the realization that the desires of your heart are God's desires too affect the way you feel about your personal desires?

4. Share a time when God fulfilled a desire or dream of your heart.

5. Many of the dreams we have when we sleep are authored by God. How does this thought make you feel?

6. Matthew 6:22-23 teaches that our eyes are the lamps for our entire body. Knowing this, can you attribute the neglect to guard your eyes to any nightmares you have had (or may currently have with regularity)?

7. What are the three purposes for having a God-dream?

8. Do you agree that it is important to be selective about who you share your dreams with? Why or why not?

9. Have you had someone in your life who you needed to remove from your inner circle because he / she was a hindrance to your growth as a child of God? What were the circumstances?

Prayer

Daddy God, I thank you for being the author of my dreams and desires. I now realize that one of the ways You speak into my faith is through dreams. In the past, I have given little regard to my dreams. Therefore, I have unknowingly disregarded important details that You desired to reveal to me. My eyes and ears are open now. Speak, Father, I am listening. . .
In Jesus' Name I pray. Amen.

Use the space below to write any specific prayer requests you have:

Your faith journey begins. . .

In Acts 16:30, a Roman jailer asks Paul and Silas, "Sirs, what must I do to be saved?" Perhaps you are pondering this same question in your own mind right now?

Many have heard about Jesus. You may even know a little about Him. Maybe you grew up going to church? But, knowing ABOUT Jesus and attending church will not save you. Everyone enters this world with a sin nature and the ONLY way to be redeemed back into proper relationship with our creator, God, is through acceptance of His Son, Jesus. My friend, we all have to make that personal choice to accept Jesus as our Savior and Lord.

The Bible tells us in John 6:44(a) that, "No one can come to Me (Jesus) unless the Father who sent Me draws them to Me." That nudging you feel right now is Holy Spirit drawing you to make a personal, heartfelt decision to accept Jesus Christ into your heart.

If you would like to invite Jesus to live inside your heart, you can do so right now. It is not the eloquent prayer you pray that matters most, but the condition of your heart. Use the prayer below as a guide and then talk to Jesus about your specific life. Confess your sins before Him and ask Holy Spirit to give you a new heart.

"Lord Jesus, I am a sinner. I have done things that go against Your good plan for my life. I am sorry. I accept Your death on the cross as the payment for my sins. I accept Your gift of eternal life. It is only through Your perfect sacrifice, Jesus, that God can look upon me and not see my sin. I believe that You died and were resurrected for me personally. My heart prayer is to become more and more like You. Strengthen me with Your Holy Spirit so that I can be a witness to others of your great goodness and mercy. I desire to begin my new life as Your child now. Amen."

Now, tell someone about your decision. Grow daily by reading His word and spending time getting to know Him. Allow Holy Spirit to begin shaping you into the man or woman He created you to be. Your blessed life starts NOW. I'm so proud of you...

"Now faith is the substance of things hoped for, the evidence of things not seen."

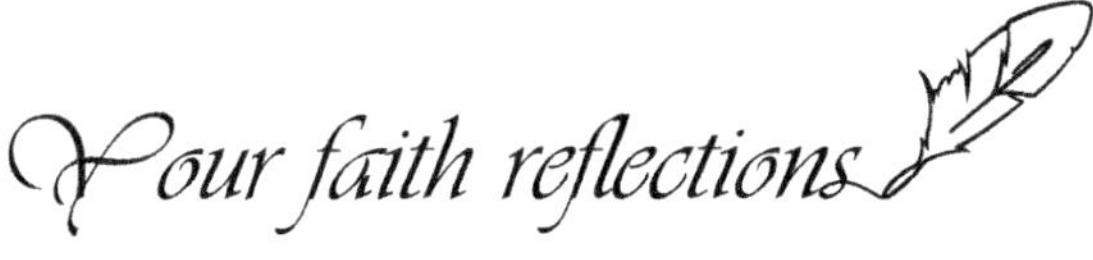

Your faith reflections

This brings us to the conclusion of *The Rhythm of Faith*. I hope you have enjoyed this journey and trust that new insights, truths, convictions, and promises have been imparted into your life through this revelation and the faithful guidance of Holy Spirit. Use the following pages to record your thoughts and to keep record of the specific faith-building events that occur in your life. Return to them time and time again to refuel and strengthen your faith. May your life be marked by supernatural, extravagant faith.

Acknowledgements

To God—for wooing me into personal, intimate relationship.
To Jesus—for personally dying for ME and salvaging my life.
To Holy Spirit—for being such a fabulous Teacher.
YOU are the best of me. My gratitude shall never cease.

To my lovey, Steve—thanks for sharing this journey with me and for being my greatest fan. Your love and support strengthen me. There is no one I'd rather do life with. You're my absolute favorite.

To my beautiful daughter, Alyse—your birth directed me to God. I will forever be grateful for how you've changed my life. I'm so proud of you and love you to pieces.

To my son, Bryce—we are kindred spirits indeed. Thanks for always being my sounding board. Your support lifts and challenges me to rise higher. You are the son of all sons.

To Nana and Dale—thank you for faithfully supporting everything I do and for always being there. I know I can always count on you.

To Krissy—you are THE BEST listener. Your friendship is PRICELESS!

To Momma Liz—for allowing HIS encouraging gift of prophecy to flow through you.

To Diana Raines Photography—your amazing talent has a way of making me look better.

To Kim Soesbee and Touch Publishing—I couldn't have done this without your expertise, talent, and friendship.

And last, but not least, thank you to everyone who has personally invested in me along the way. You know who you are and my life is a culmination of your many seeds.

Author Jeneen Kohler

Jeneen Kohler is a yielded servant and teacher in the Body of Christ. Married at the young age of seventeen, she sought salvation, restoration, and guidance in Jesus Christ for the first time. Twenty-seven years of marriage to her best friend and high school sweetheart, Steve, and two wonderful children later, God's faithful hand has guided her to a successful and fulfilling life founded on biblical truths.

As co-founder of Repairing the Breach Ministries, Inc., a licensed minister through Worldwide Missionary Evangelism, and international speaker and author, Jeneen is given to the ministry of restoration, with a heart to witness individuals restored to wholeness of spirit, soul, and body. Her ministry leans heavily on the pitfalls and triumphs of personal life experience.

As a genuinely passionate and engaging Bible teacher and writer, with more than twenty years of ministry leadership, Jeneen possesses a confident faith that the revelation and application of God's Word has the power to build strong, stable foundations that transform any life. As a result, her help-based ministry is instrumental in assisting others on their victorious journeys to becoming all that God destined them to be.

To contact Jeneen to speak at your event, visit:
www.RepairingtheBreachMinistries.org

Pg 64 - Wisdom

Wisdom is the supernatural ability to understand a situation from God's perspective; . . prov. 3:13-18

Pg 65 - "The Word of God is quick, powerful..."

Repairing The Breach Ministries, Inc.

Repairing the Breach Ministries (RTBM) is called to REACH the hurting, hopeless, and lost through benevolent ministry.

We are:

- Spreading the gospel
- Feeding the homeless
- Caring and providing for orphans and widows
- Aiding those in temporary life crisis
- Financially assisting other leaders and evangelical ministries
- Equipping people with truth

RTBM is called to REPAIR the broken areas with His love and RESTORE hope and destiny as we satisfy the emotional, physical, and spiritual needs of mankind.

Visit our website to learn more about our ministry, to donate, or to connect with RTBM.

RepairingtheBreachMinistries.org

Repairing the Breach Ministries, Inc. is a registered 501(c)3 non-profit organization.

God whatever you have for my life, put that desire in my heart.

Lord, help me to know "Your" heart.

"Lord, What Do You Desire For Me?

Fill Me With the desires of Your heart for my life.

Pg 62

"He drew me all to Himself and renovated my Life".

CPSIA information can be obtained at www.ICGtesting.com
Printed in the USA
BVOW11s1228310715

411224BV00003BA/6/P